Twice Blessed

First Century Christians in a Twenty-First Century World

J O S E P H   A .   M C G E E

WESTBOW
P R E S S®
A DIVISION OF THOMAS NELSON
& ZONDERVAN

WestBow Press books may be ordered through booksellers or by contacting:

WestBow Press
A Division of Thomas Nelson & Zondervan
1663 Liberty Drive
Bloomington, IN 47403
www.westbowpress.com
844-714-3454

All Scripture quotations are taken from The Holy Bible, New International Version®, NIV® Copyright © 1973, 1978, 1984, 2011 by Biblica, Inc.® Used by permission. All rights reserved worldwide.

ISBN: 978-1-6642-5369-8 (sc)
ISBN: 978-1-6642-5370-4 (hc)
ISBN: 978-1-6642-5368-1 (e)

Library of Congress Control Number: 2021925408

Print information available on the last page.

WestBow Press rev. date: 1/22/2022

Very special thanks to my beautiful wife, Kat, who has stood by me for better, for worse, for richer, for poorer, in sickness and in health, for forty-five years.

Thanks to Marla Coffee for her help, to Staci and Abby of Snow Tree Media, and to my friends in home church.

Special thanks to all my friends at the Emergency Shelter of Northern Kentucky.

And thanks to God, from whom all blessings flow.

To the brave people who courageously speak truth to power—and to my college friend, who became the first man I knew who died for it. May the Spirit of Truth give them peace. Like the man born blind, they are sent, but the unspiritual and worldly people can neither see the truth nor understand. Their courage sustains us all.

In the Bible, in the book of John, Jesus meets a man born blind and gives him sight. The man born blind is questioned by the ruling priests and the learned Pharisees, who fear and suppress any new teachings and persecute those who follow Jesus. They kept asking what Jesus did and how He was able to give sight to a man born blind. Under repeated questioning:

The man answered, "Now that is remarkable! You don't know where he comes from, yet he opened my eyes. We know that God does not listen to sinners. He listens to the Godly person who does His will. Nobody has ever heard of opening the eyes of a man born blind. If this man were not from God, he could do nothing."

To this they replied, "You were steeped in sin at birth! How dare you lecture us!" And they threw him out.

Jesus heard that they had thrown him out and when he had found him, he said, "Do you believe in the Son of Man?"

"Who is he, sir?" the man asked. "Tell me so that I may believe in him."

Jesus said, "You have now seen him; in fact, he is the one speaking with you."

Then the man said, "Lord, I believe," and he worshipped him. (John 9:30–38)

Contents

Preface

Twenty years ago, I joined a mainstream institutional church. I was not a saved Christian. I was a seeker, trying to understand. I said the words I was supposed to say and tried as hard as I could to believe them. This book is intended to be the book I would have wanted someone to give me before they let me join, then tested me to see if I fully understood it. Later, when I got cancer, it is one of the books I wish might have been available to me, to help me understand suffering, death, and loss.

Many things about the institutional churches need repair. I could suggest improvements, but huge organizations are not very approachable. So, I go to a home church, a small group of saved Christians meeting in members' houses. No one asks me for money, so instead, I donate comparable amounts to a local homeless shelter, where I volunteer a few nights a week. Why are these things so?

Twenty-first century religious institutions are worldly, and there is no greater proof than their constant demands for money, and investment of the money, in worldly buildings, finery, and physical objects—and, in some instances, highly compensated pastors and teachers. This leads to more demands for money, money that could be used for the poor, money beyond the needs of a Godly assembly. It is like the "Corban" practice in Mark 7, which will be explained later in this book.

On the other hand, I think these issues are really a problem because of religious organizations filling their pews with seekers and people who are not saved but think they are "covered" by membership in their "church" organization; and people who believe, but are not really growing in faith. So, as a result, they do not understand that Christ wants each of us to be surrendered 100 percent to Him and to put aside our worldly desires for Him. Sin (worldly desire) is the master of the sinner, and you cannot serve two masters. Realizing we cannot magically eliminate desire all at once, we work on it as long as we live, as best we can, with God's help. But if a person has not first come to a profound belief, the effort is fruitless; we first need the spiritual *transformation,*[1] which comes with complete surrender to Christ and cannot be obtained in any other way. This may happen all at once or over a long time, as faith grows.

The day-to-day operations of the church are worldly, and there is a lot of emphasis on increasing membership, attendance, and donations. A few attend weekly Bible study groups. But there are also cliques, church politics, and unabashed deference to big donors. And there is very little emphasis on subjects like how to respond to personal crises in a Biblical way. Some ministers are very good at helping people through a crisis, but in a large congregation, you have to seek them out. So a man may commit suicide, and no one may have expected anything or ever known he needed help.

I will say this for the mainstream Church: the Gospel is there if you can see through the dogma and ritual and worldliness, and many have and have found Jesus Christ this way. But I think it is imperative they get their mind off things like money and worldly artifacts, politics, arguments over trivia and ritual—and focus on making sure every member is saved, or at least is actively seeking Christ. I really don't think it's possible. How intimately can you know 400 or 500 people in a congregation to assist and support one another's spiritual needs? I sat in the same pew every Sunday for twenty years and yet was uncomfortable talking about the experiences that I wrote about in my first book, *I, Witness.*

The Bible now is often taught in a fractured form. It is made complicated. The truth is that it is *simple* and anyone of sound mind

---

[1] 1 The Greek word metanoia, in many passages is translated "repentance" in many Bibles. But in context I think the better would be transformed mind. Meta means "beyond" or "after" and nous, the root word means mind. The nature of the transformation is *spiritual.* See for example 1 Cor. Ch. 2. The transformation is the gift of spiritual awakening that comes to people who truly believe in Christ.

can understand it. But it requires a deep belief, in one's heart, not mere repetitions and rituals. Without *belief*, these are useless. (See Hebrews 4:1–3.) Another reason this is so important is that we are tested, sifted, and shaken. People die who we love, even our children. There are fires, floods, famines, wars, and pandemics—also, cancer, job loss, divorce, business failure, bankruptcy, homelessness, all things that can test a person to the core. How do we respond? Do we lose faith because we swallow the lie that "a just God would not allow these things to happen to nice people?" Read on and you will see that this is a lie; propaganda from the atheist cult, and from Satan!

Do we fall into bitterness and depression? Are we swallowing pills or wine because we are unable to accept our present situation? Weak faith is like watery coffee—useless. Everything difficult that happens is also a *test*. It is never just about the challenge; it's always about how we respond. The toilet paper panic of 2020 was a perfect example. The next time, it could be food. Can you respond as a Christian, trusting in God, resisting the temptation to hoard food? Christ *will* provide for us, as He did me with a prescription for my personal crises.

Christ also demands that we love one another—that means a sincere love for all the members of the congregation. Paul makes it clear that this is imperative. We are the body of Christ. When one hurts, we all hurt. When one needs anything, we all help. When others in the community have needs, our neighbors, we help them as well out of genuine compassion, not to assuage our feelings of shame and guilt.

Another problem with anything less than deep belief and surrender is that you cannot fool the Risen Lord! He sees right through you. He knows everything about you, and nothing is hidden. He demonstrated this to me in a very dramatic way as is recapitulated in the appendix of this book. He wants us to be "all-in."

Fortunately, we *can* all get there. We must take stock of ourselves, look deeply into ourselves and see our sin and accept its sinfulness, ditch all of our excuses and justifications and moral relativism, see it as it is. We are all sinners! If you are anything at all like me, this inner journey will be hard and sickening. You will be brought to your knees, realizing it and, kneeling at the foot of the cross, crying "Jesus! Help me!" *This is exactly how I felt it.* It is a terrible pain, but if we bear it, it is tremendously fruitful. It will change your life. This is how I am able with the help of the Holy Spirit to be at peace with two cancers and all the problems of the worldly existence.

Christ is the *center* of a Christian life. A Christian begins and ends his days to the extent practicable with prayer and meditation. Giving is a blessing, sacrifice an honor, service an opportunity—all done out of love for Christ and our fellowman. And, as well as he can he always proclaims the risen Christ, sometimes in a loud voice, sometimes a gentle word or an act of kindness. He is our Risen Lord; Him only do we serve. And I humbly ask the Holy Spirit to help me day by day to grow into this person.

We must count the cost. Christians are *guaranteed* suffering in His name. In much of the world the cost of the cross is death at the hands of unbelievers. Until I read their stories, I did not fully understand what a first-century Christian life was like. Now, in the twenty-first century, more than 100,000 people a year are killed, kneeling in the dirt with their families just for being followers—unwilling to renounce faith in Christ. We must make the choice in advance and pray on it frequently, if the time ever comes, that the Holy Spirit give us the strength to accept it. See Luke 21:10–20. Of course, this is not demanded of most of us, unless we live in third-world countries. But we may be ridiculed, we may lose "friends," and we may be blocked on social media. We might even lose our job or be denied other opportunities because we speak boldly that Jesus is Lord, or because we speak out in other ways. We may be told that this is inappropriate. We don't discuss religion or politics. It's not polite. I respond, "So sorry. I was not discussing religion or politics; I was merely stating a fact." So, the choice to be *all-in* means, "No, I am not going to stop talking when someone asks a question," the real answer to which is, Jesus. I am not willing to varnish over the answer. Nor am I willing to go along with political correctness or other things I know are false. I used to be that kind of person, to my shame, but since I met Him, I cannot.

The choice is liberating. Much of our fear and anxiety is unnecessary. This worldly body was a free gift. It dies. We must prepare in our minds to let it go, along with all else in the worldly realm. We did nothing to earn the blood of Yeshua on the cross, shed for us willingly, out of love.

It was a free gift. We are children of light, spirits, and we belong to the spiritual realm. This life was given to perfect us to the *greater* realm, according to God's plan. Therefore, rejoice and be glad in it.

Here is what I hope to show you in this book:

1. A Christian explanation of why people get "stuck" or feel they "can't ever get anywhere" and a Christian prescription for that malady.
2. A simple way for everyone to understand the *whole* Bible so there is a framework in which to put all the stories and wisdom and solve the seeming paradoxes (which are not really paradoxes if you understand the big picture).
3. A series of essays on how the Bible really teaches us to live as Christian brothers and sisters.
4. A way to understand suffering and death so they make sense and are not seen as meaningless cruelty to those who believe.

I know this is a hefty boast, and I hope the book lives up to it. If it does, it is God through, the Holy Spirit. I, like everyone else, am just another sinner.

Blessings and peace.

PART ONE

How We Get Stuck,
and a Christian Approach
to Getting Un-stuck[2]

---

[2] I am not asserting that this is an answer to all psychological problems, or that psychology can't be useful. One of the most common problems I see in a lot of people is dissatisfaction with their present circumstances, disappointment over a perceived lack of achievement in life, or the feeling of constantly being at the mercy of things they cannot control. Over time, these things can leave a person vulnerable to depression, chronic anxiety, and even lead to suicide in some people. Many of them keep coming back to saying they feel "stuck" or that they can't ever seem to "get anywhere." Others wonder why their lives just aren't what they are "supposed" to be. I think Christians have some good alternatives for these situations.

Why "First-Century Christians in the Twenty-First Century?"

Before my *metanoia* (Greek, "change of mind" or "change of heart"[3]), I was unable to understand the Bible. It was as if the veil of Moses covered my eyes (see 2 Corinthians 3:14). This is very strange to me, because while I may not speak Greek or Hebrew, my comprehension of written English is extremely high. I had a full scholarship and straight As in law school, and I practiced law for many years, writing briefs, memoranda, and legal opinions that were accepted by courts at all levels.

One of the reasons the Bible is hard to understsnd is the way churches conduct their teaching. We sit in the pews and listen to what one man or woman says. We do not discuss; we don't do homework. Second, the reading on Sunday is usually a couple of short excerpts—a few verses from the Old Testament, a few from a Gospel, and a short passage from an Epistle. All this takes five minutes because they do not want to "bore you" with overmuch Scripture. Then there's a twenty-minute homily, a few songs, the collection, and the Lord's Prayer, and then you can get home in time for football on TV.

But when my eyes were opened, I *really* read the Bible. Since I was trained in the law, I studied and analyzed it as I would a legal document or case law. For the first time, I was able to read it *as written*. The Holy Spirit showed me the good news in bold. I was almost afraid to read

---

[3] This word is translated as "repentance" in many Bible versions. It can also mean "beyond-thought." A different Greek word, *metamelomai*, is more accurately the word for "repentance." What is beyond-thought? It is part transformation of mind and part spiritual sight. These things have huge implications for the practicing Christian.

on, afraid my "good news" was not real; but contrarily, I found the whole Bible supported it 100 percent. It is *all* good news. It is easy to understand, and you don't really need anyone else to interpret it for you. It just isn't taught that way.

It is valuable to have friends with greater learning to discuss it with and to share teachings, revelations, and experiences. There is more than one meaning to almost every part, the superficial and the deeper, the immediate and the future, the general and the personal. God led me to a dedicated group that formed a home church, and we meet as often as we can, even during the pandemic. They have helped me to learn these things. As I said, my intent is to put together what I wish I had known twenty years ago, but I have found out now by really reading the Bible, with God's help and a few friends.

One point (and some will hate this): the Bible contains history, but it also contains stories, allegories, parables, figures of speech, idioms, and poetry. Due to the passage of time and changes in the world and in culture and language, some of these are not altogether clearly demarcated. But one must use one's ability to discern. My point is that the "hyperliteralism" of some people is not a fair reading. So the Bible may say a "thousand years" and mean that—exactly to the day—or it may mean "a very long time." You, *with* the Holy Spirit, are to use your *discernment* to decide for *yourself* (see Romans 14). None of these issues detracts one iota from the overall meaning of the Bible, but they do provide fodder for the God-hating atheists and the "weak believers," who are compelled to demand everyone think alike and to attack you on Facebook. Ignore them. Everything in the Bible is true. Some may be historical, while others may be stories or illustrations, like the parables of Jesus.[4]

I also have a disagreement with text proofing. People take out of context verses or short passages that appear to say something when read and use them to prove a point that is not what the author or speaker

---

[4] These negative-oriented people focus so much attention on arguments about the books of Genesis and Revelation, one has to wonder whether they have read what lies between. For most people, the truth of the gospel will do a lot more to make life better than arguing over the events of the distant past and future! If you see these comments on Facebook, I suggest you simply ignore them and focus on living a Christian life today.

intended.[5] This includes not only the entire passage, chapter, or book but also the who, what, when, where, and why questions. Who was the speaker, and who was the audience? What was the full subject of the discussion? What were the full circumstances? What was the motivation? Were there idioms and figures of speech, such as dramatic overstatement, to emphasize a point? All these must be prayerfully considered in light of the overall message of the Bible.[6] I can tell you right now that, taken as a whole, the entire Bible is good news. The encapsulated message is "for God so loved the world that He gave His only begotten Son that men might not perish but have everlasting life" (John 3:16). Anything inconsistent with that is a misinterpretation. Everyone can be saved. Jesus said, "All things are possible with God" (Mark 10:27). Amen. One example of how people use text proofing is by interpreting John 6:44 in support of an inflexible view of predestination. It states that no one can come to Christ unless the Father calls them, but it does not state under what circumstances God, the Sovereign, will do so, or that He might not wait for another time with some people, for reasons we do not know. Furthermore, it does not negate the opportunity for free will to play its part. Finally, the subject under discussion was not free will or predestination but salvation. People can read all sorts of implications into it that simply are not there. If you are reading this book, you *are* being called.

I wish to make clear, however, that the entire Bible is *one* story. God has *one* plan, which is what He always intended. There is not and never has been any plan B. From the fall to the resurrection; from Melchizedek to Yeshua, the high priest forever; from the ram whose horn was caught in the thicket to the blood on the cross, it has all been unity. It all fits. It all makes sense. It is not a "mystery"—not since Christ was raised from the dead. And those who trust in Him *will* be raised at the last day (John 6:40).

We are spirit; God is spirit. We are required and expected to walk in His footsteps, however painful, however far. We are *guaranteed* suffering for His sake. This is not "unfair." He asks no more of us than He gave of

---

[5] The technical term for this is *eisegesis*. But it is taking verses and reading into them one's own ideas.

[6] The term for this is *exegesis*, from the Greek word meaning "to draw out"; we seek always to extract the full meaning of everything in the Bible.

Himself. He lived homeless. He was reviled and accused, and although he was innocent, He was tried, convicted, and executed.

In three-quarters of the world, Christians can suffer the same fate: we can be demoted to second-class citizens, we can be slandered, or we can be imprisoned, tortured, and killed for the cross. And worse is coming. But the Bible says "fear not"; those who can harm the flesh cannot harm the spirit. Amen.

If we look for it, the Bible tells us exactly how to live. And the Holy Spirit guides and teaches us; it empowers us. In fact, it is our superpower. We do things we "can't" do; we go places we are afraid to go; we make things happen. And everywhere we go, we plant seeds of the Gospel. Remember though, *we* cannot do these things; only the Holy Spirit, living in us, is able to do them. No one may boast before God.

Regarding our difficulties in life, the Bible teaches us their *meaning*. Gold is refined in fire. Ore is placed in a crucible, the metal comes out, and the rest, the dross, is thrown away. This is our purification. I can accept my situation with cancer and all that goes with it because I know it is how I will be *purified*. The same is also true of our inner struggles and mental anguish, our search for God, and our regrets about the past.

We are also *tested* to make sure our faith is strong. Whatever happens, it is not about the thing that happens, be it fire, flood, famine, pandemic, or persecution. It is always about how we choose to respond—either as Christians, putting others first and always seeking the Lord—or as fools running to Walmart to grab up all the TP.

Christ forgives and takes away the burdens of the past mistakes and frees us to follow Him. He assures us of a future where we will not be punished for them (see John 5:24). "Today, if you hear his voice, do not harden your hearts" (Hebrews 3:7). Therefore, listen for His voice in your prayer time and in reading His Word. Try to let God guide everything you do, as well as you can. Pray to continue to live for Him and for humankind. Pray to serve as a servant those less fortunate. Do not pose as a benefactor, but let the Holy Spirit work through you.

And please be *happy*! We were given this life here in the flesh as a gift and did nothing to earn it. We did nothing to earn the gift of Christ's blood to save us from our mistakes. It is all a gift. What is there to be unhappy about?

Twice Blessed

Life is great, and death is not the end, so why doesn't it always feel that way?

Last night, I was lucky. I saw several people whom I really like, two I had not seen in person for almost a year thanks to the pandemic. We talked a bit, but I didn't offer them a book for fear they would take it personally, being part of the mainstream institutional church I had left.[7] Maybe I was wrong about that. I know they are Godly people. One, though, a homeless boy of twenty-four years old, I did give it to. I hope he reads it. I know he wants to get his life on a better path.

Also, I saw another homeless friend with whom I had been discussing parts of the book. He is a kindhearted and wise man of the street. Someone had taken his backpack and his book. And one does wonder. Who steals from a homeless person? Most of our local homeless stick together and cooperate or help one another. Some may steal cash or easily sellable items due to addictions they cannot control, but the pack is the sum of everything a person has in this world— clothing, a blanket or a bedroll, sometimes a knife, a poncho for rain. Spare socks. Medicine. It is cruel. But my friend has learned to roll with the punches, even though they hurt at the time, having a kind of strength one gets only by suffering. Also, he is a Christian, and he prays for all of us. No, he does not "have it all worked out," but at least he knows that. And so, he prays and tries to help who he can, and to me, he stands tall even with his problems and weaknesses, for I also

---

[7] My first book, *I, Witness*.

know my problems and weaknesses, and they are as many and as bad as anyone's. It is here in the knowledge of our brokenness that people can come together honestly.

The street people—those who have been in and out of shelters and jails and lived under bridges for years—have many different stories. Many grew up in circumstances of abuse and neglect. Many were foster kids. Many have addictions. Sometimes they are second- or third-generation addicts or alcoholics. Others have been in and out of jails and prisons, mostly for minor offenses or for possession of substances they are addicted to. And yet, many believe in God and in Jesus Christ. Some have been saved and baptized. Some are trying to get out of the life, but bad records, bad credit, low wages, gentrification of neighborhoods, and prejudice have made it very difficult. Nevertheless, I have found that they are more reachable with the Gospel than the well-to-do, the satisfied people for whom church occupies an hour per week, and the decidedly secular, who see them and say, "Why bother?" Why is this the case?

The reason is obvious to me. (Bear with me, as I must explain a couple of things first.) The Old Testament prophets predicted two versions of the Messiah—one who suffers and one who is the king. This was the reason John (the Baptist) asked whether Jesus was the Messiah or whether they should expect another. God revealed his plan fully in the resurrection. Yeshua (Jesus) was both. He was first impoverished, homeless, spiritual, crucified; then raised, glorified, and filled with power, holding the keys of the kingdom and seated in the seat of judgment, next to the Father (YHWH), who will return in power and glory at the end of time and raise us anew.

But the poor were *always* a special case to him. The orphan, the widow, the beggar, the blind, the crippled (see Isaiah 1:11–23). Christ saw their suffering; He saw their humility. I have found they are more likely not to think they are already perfect and know everything.

"You say, 'I am rich; I have acquired wealth and I do not need a thing.' But you do not realize that you are wretched, pitiful, poor, blind and naked" (Revelation 3:17). If you are a middle-class American in the twenty-first century, doesn't this describe so many people you know? A nice suburban home, three cars, teenagers in private school, but in many ways unhappy, dissatisfied, anxious, and depressed? The homeless are more likely to understand that their lives are in a state of disrepair, and many are looking for hope. Less pride, more openness to be reached.

Suffering, in addition to the knowledge that one's life is in need of repair, is more profound than any knowledge we may glean from a yoga class or a self-improvement book; it can bring a person kneeling at the foot of the cross, ready to surrender to the Benevolent King. This is why it is so hard for a "rich" man to enter the kingdom of heaven.

Christ admonished the church in Laodicea to buy from him gold refined by fire so they could become rich (Revelation 3:18). It is not enough for comfortable, self-satisfied people to go to church, put money in the collection plate, and volunteer once a month with the food distribution, to lead a secular life the remaining time. Sorry, but that is too easy. It's not enough to offer a five-minute prayer once a day and "go to church" on Sunday (the twenty-first century way.) But don't feel too bad. Jesus said, "Those whom I love I rebuke and discipline. So be earnest and repent" (Revelation 3:19). If you already believe in Him, it is not a long way to go, and He loves you. Jesus wants us to be *all-in*. What might that look like? First, we must realize what we are and what we are not. We see a mirror in the poor, the homeless, the orphan, the prisoner. They are not "other"; they are us!

Seeing the truth and being honest with ourselves, we can come clean, and in the right frame of mind, we can come to Him. For, unequivocally, *every* life needs repair. Not only have we all fallen short of God's glory (Romans 3:10–18), but the majority of us live lives more devoted to things than to people, more devoted to what we call our *lifestyle* than to Jesus Christ. This makes us idolaters, even if we don't know it.

We need to think long and hard about how safe we are in America. Yes, it's nice to be safe. But in many countries, merely being Christian openly is grounds for arrest, imprisonment, torture, and execution. Scores of people die every day in the persecuted lands simply for refusing to renounce their faith. Are we ready for that? Read up on this. Join Voice of the Martyrs.[8] People give their lives just to take Communion. So, if your Communion is not symbolic of unity with them, what is it?

---

[8] Voice of the Martyrs is an organization that helps Christians in persecuted countries.

"Take up your cross and follow me!" (Luke 14:28). Decide in your heart whether you would be willing to suffer and die for the One who suffered and died for you. Then, if you are honest with yourself, you will have to pray for the Holy Spirit to help you develop a deeper faith; to make you stand when you cannot stand on your own. Very few are ready for this. I know it is God, through faith, who empowers such things, not people on their own. Living the Gospel is not easy. Not that this will be demanded of most Americans; nor should we go looking for it (but you may be unfriended a lot on Facebook).

You say, "Boy, that's kind of dire," but it is also liberating. It blows away a lot of our anxiety about the future to realize that we are so committed that we are committed to live and die for something greater than ourselves, knowing absolutely that Jesus has our back. To understand that we can make a conscious decision to be that person. For that is what it is—a conscious decision, made ahead of time, to give Him our all and renewed daily in prayer. But Christ demands real commitment from His followers. He willingly laid down His life for me. This stuff is all serious. We are going to die in the flesh. Everyone is going to die. We all came into this world naked and bloody and screaming, and many go out the same way. Everyone simply ignores those facts most of the time. First-century Christians lived it.

It also means that if God calls us, we must be willing to go. God called me to work among the homeless through the pandemic. I am seventy-four years old. There is a risk. In *I, Witness*, I noted that Jonah was afraid to do what God wanted. Sure, it was scary, but as I also realized, we are in the valley of the shadow of death from the moment of conception (especially these days). But we are also resting in God's gentle hands the whole time. He is our Father, and He cares for us. And even if He sends us into the lion's den, He goes in with us.

So, first-century Christians in the twenty-first century are those who are attempting to live as close to the realities, and to the Bible as written, as we can, sometimes throwing off trappings and doctrines of the modern Church and instead seeking in prayer daily the guidance and power of the Holy Spirit. We do not necessarily subscribe to any organized religion. We do not all tithe in the stone buildings.[9] Rather, we do everything we can to help humanity and to spread the Gospel and to follow God's callings. We keep a healthy respect for the dangers of this evil time, but we speak boldly, we walk in dangerous places, and we rely on God as our backup.

---

[9] This is not universal. Some do still go to their organized churches and perform its rituals and pay its tithes. There are no set requirements except to be saved and understand we have to be fully committed to Him.

Stuck

In *I, Witness*, I described some of the ways I got stuck and areas where I struggled all my life. Also, I posted on deepfaithjourney.com other people's testimonies of being stuck. It was Christ, I explained, who freed me, and others have testified how He freed them.

The reason I had such a hard time accepting the diagnosis of cancer and the prospect of death was that my mind was focusing on things that existed in the material realm exclusively. For thirty years, I had been overly focused on my career, working at first six and a half days every week, missing a lot of important things at home and subjecting myself to suffering depression and anxiety to provide, looking to an imaginary future where we would all be happy. After I lost a kidney to a blood clot in 2010, I finally decided that I would retire as soon as I could, but I imagined that I was "entitled" to a long, happy retired life. Now I had stage-4 cancer. It's not fair. I was a "Christian" and, I had worked hard all my life, but my dreams were being taken away from me. Why? Why did I sacrifice so much of my life sitting at my desk, poring over documents, depositions, and cases instead of playing with my kids? I did spend time with them as much as I could, but I felt I had to get ahead. I had to win. I had to become "successful."

When I retired, I put all my diplomas and awards in a box and walked out of the office with a lump in my throat. I took the box home and placed it in a closet. It is still sitting there exactly where it was seven and a half years ago. When I die, my family will probably take it out and divide it up, and store bits of it in their own respective closets, throwing out the rest. *This is the fate of secular man, he who does not live a spiritual life.*

Many of us, even those who have now been persuaded of the Spirit and of the Lordship of Christ, get "stuck." It is a terrible thing, forever ruminating about the past and things that "might have been," forever worried about the possible futures in our minds, always focused on our imperfections or on how we imagine ourselves in the future, perpetually seeking ways to be relieved temporarily from the heart ache of the past—lost loves, lost dreams, lost people. We fear that in the end we are "failures," aware that after so many years, we have not achieved whatever we once imagined we would by now. Anxious yet unable even to name what we are anxious about—an unnamed dread located in our imagined "future," knotting up in the pit of our stomachs.

Do any of these sound familiar?

And one cannot help feeling a bit of self-pity at the "unfairness" of it all. After all, others seem to be so happy, so why has God visited these afflictions on me? I am not an especially awful person. And to comfort ourselves, we use alcohol or drugs, escape to fantasy, focus on sports on TV, self-medicate, seek psychiatry, or search in vain for answers. The common feature of all these mental water tortures is that they are founded on a premise that is false, has always been false, and will always be false: the idea that "I" am the thing that matters.

By this, I mean the "I" we all see in our minds. The worldly self. The expectation that I must "move forward" in life to "succeed," to be "more," or to satisfy some other arbitrary measure to be more successful than I am at present. Of course, then, if I do not, or if there are setbacks, I will be plagued by the perception that I never seem to "get anywhere." It is the idea that my plans for my life are the plan, and if they don't succeed, I will be a "failure," a "loser," or a "bad" person.

All this is incorrect thinking.

The struggle also results in a conflict within every Christian believer (Romans 7:7–25). The mind, the will, and the spirit wish to do only what is good. But the flesh (or the worldly self) seeks to satisfy itself and its worldly wants. Additionally, this world has so many ways to please the flesh that we cannot always avoid them. Further, without some of them, we cannot live even a Godly life.

Without oxygen, water, and food, we die. Without sex, we cannot reproduce. Without taking action to shelter ourselves, we perish.

Making matters more challenging is that God has arranged our brain chemistry to incentivize the things necessary to live, to be healthy, and to reproduce abundantly. The feel-good brain chemicals—serotonin, dopamine, and oxytocin—are arranged to get us to do the things God intended, like finding food and reproducing. Adrenaline was given to help us when faced with danger.

However, all forms of unhealthy indulgence—for example, sensual pleasures, chemical substances, gambling—release large amounts of the same chemicals. Therefore, we need to know there is a biological reason people become "slaves to sin" (Romans 6:16–18).

Those brain chemicals God has given us to help us are also used by the devil to trap people. It is true that a little dopamine makes us feel good, but exogenous chemical stimulation of dopamine release (fancy talk for taking drugs and alcohol) wears off, leaving us feeling depressed, often without knowing why, and concluding that because of this, life itself is against us. Add to that our situational challenges—loss, loneliness, unemployment, homelessness, and illness —and we formulate thought patterns that support the point of view that life is unfair, that we have been singled out, or that we are victims (i.e., bad thinking).

Alternatively, we may believe that money is the answer and that if we keep playing the game, eventually our luck will change and we will be transformed from "loser" to "winner." All our dreams will come true. Those who are more fortunate may endlessly pursue wealth and prosperity without any thought to spiritual matters. I believe that such people are harder to persuade about Jesus than the homeless because they think they were selected to be successful or, worse, that everything in life is determined by merit. Fortunately, this is not the case, as we are all sinners. Alternatively, some may feel intense guilt and seek to assuage this by giving money, but they continue to experience the pangs of a guilty conscience, drinking and pursuing other bad habits to quell the discomfort and never understanding the reasons for it. All of these ideas are Satan's ideas, traps he sets for people.

None of the unhealthy habits, including the idolatry of "success," can ever lead to lasting happiness; they merely pile up, resulting in unending human misery and death. And the death is also the death of the spirit and the loss of the opportunity for continuous life through Christ.

Sexual addiction leads to a trail of tears, broken relationships, unwanted children, betrayal, poverty, and often alcoholism and other addictions, disease, and death.

Substance abuse leads to loss of control over one's actions and life, loss of family, loss of friends, theft, murder, imprisonment, and death.

Overindulgence of other kinds lead to every sort of human misery and depravity and ultimately to death.

The idolatry of "success" is worship of self, which is idolatry and merits damnation as much as other sins we may look upon with disgust! And it leads to loss of the chances to maximize our time here, to unhealthy habits, and to heart attacks, depression, suicide, and death.[10]

But what leads to freedom, happiness, and life? We may answer this question by deciding *who or what to serve.* Because everyone serves something. If you do not make a conscious choice, the body of flesh (worldly self) makes the choice for you. If you go any way the wind blows, eventually, you will wind up on the rocks, and the ocean of life will tear you to pieces a little at a time. I have watched many people be destroyed in the seventy-plus years I have been on this earth; however, no one was destroyed who did not first destroy himself.

People destroy themselves because of fickle lovers. They destroy themselves over the failure to obtain what they want or what they think they should have. They destroy themselves seeking the approval of others, even of cruel parents and even after these parents are no longer living. They destroy themselves with drink and with drugs and with sin in pursuit of what they think will make them happy or to alleviate feelings of guilt, shame, and inadequacy. No one whose life is built around these pursuits will ever be genuinely happy. Our physical looks fade. Money comes and goes. You can lose everything in a heartbeat. People drown in a sea of booze and disappointment and tears.

Even philanthropists who seek to leave a legacy by having their name on the cornerstone of a building are eventually forgotten. You may buy a monument to yourself through charity, but in one hundred

---

[10] See also Ecclesiastes 2:1-22. All worldly pursuits are fruitless in the end!

years, no one will care much. People, sadly, think they can gamble and steal their way to happiness. Or work their way to happiness. It all fails. What is left? The cornerstone the worldly men reject: Jesus Christ. The one hope that does not fail.

"The one who believes in him will never be put to shame" (Romans 9:33).[11]

With Him, the past that haunts you has been erased. Your slate has been wiped clean. Your sins are forgiven completely. Because of the blood He shed, we have been given a fresh start. "In Him it has always been always 'yes'" (2 Corinthians 1:19–20). The flesh wants what it wants, but the mind has been reformed to understand that we are spiritual beings and have been persuaded that Jesus Christ is Lord and that God has raised him from the dead (Romans 10:9). Therefore, we are baptized into the death and resurrection of Jesus and given eternal life (Romans 6:1–5; John 5:24).

But the spirit is still housed in the tent of flesh as long as we are here. As Paul points to in Romans 8, the spirit and the flesh are mutually opposed. The flesh seeks to retain the spirit, for without it, the flesh dies. Yet the spirit longs to be free. What of the future? He has sealed you with the Holy Spirit (2 Corinthians 1:21–22). The flesh may be killed, but the spirit will live continually. Amen.

Now, some people hear me say these things and believe I am preaching "religion." I am not! To me, "religion" is the trappings people attached to it for human purposes. I'm not saying religion is bad or wrong. For many people, they seem to need to belong to a "religion" or religious organization. They need rules and order.

Christ said, "All who have come before me are thieves and robbers" (John 10:8). Indeed. And many who came later are as well. I belonged to a church organization for twenty years, and assumed I was "covered" for my sins. But when I needed it most, it was useless to save me. Many people in such organizations are saved. But that is because through all the trappings of "religion" they have found Jesus Christ and believed in him wholeheartedly. And having done so, it does not matter whether they follow ritual or not (John 5:24). They must lead Godly lives. But,

---

[11] Other translations say "trusts."

neither Baptism nor Communion nor Last Rites nor internment in hallowed ground is necessary for salvation. Salvation comes by having belief (John 6:29). Receiving the spiritual sight and eternal life are gifts He gives to those who sincerely believe in Him. However, the belief must be deep, heartfelt, sincere, and without reservation—a conviction to die for.[12]

The "way" (what first-century Christians called themselves) exists, in part, for us to meet, encourage, exhort, exchange, and build up that belief—by faith, by works, by preaching, by prayer and fasting and meditation, and by reading the Scripture. Because Satan will come at all hours to try to confuse one and snatch away that which one has attained.

There are two main reasons I continue to publish these thoughts.

1. Unsaved people reject "religion" because they can see much of it is unspiritual, worldly, and contrived. They see the manmade trappings as arbitrary and contrived because they *are*. And people see the worldliness of all the churches in the constant demands for cash. And if we are just going through the motions, our children also see that and reject it.

2. Even the saved get confused and the devil seeks always to confuse that which would save them—and to destroy them. He is a liar and a destroyer and uses every kind of trick to harm people in their mind and body and circumstances. Therefore, most of us need continual mutual support and reassurance. In the first century, many believers met daily. And now, our Church organizations have been closed for an entire year! And they have accepted this!

To all who have attained this faith in the risen Christ, I propose that we are God's instruments. I pray, do not be ashamed to tell others your personal salvation story, admitting humbly that you too were once lost in sin and that you now help others to become strong in faith in every way. There is no virtue in pretending to have it all worked out. I think

---

[12] This does not mean saved people will not have moments of doubt. The devil always tries to trick us, like Peter walking on the water (Matthew 14:23–33). We learn ways to deal with these.

we need to continually hear these things from others to keep strong in our own faith. Also, I believe we should testify openly. This does not mean public confession of sin, but I won't give in to people who say it is impolite to discuss what they call "religion" openly, as a normal part of conversation, or to confine it to "church." The devil is the author of these lies; he just wants to suppress the truth of the Gospel!

For those who have not yet been saved, I say, listen to the stories of those who have. Pray for spiritual sight. There is another reality beyond this one. It is as real as the one we are in and can see with the eyes of flesh. Rather than the trappings of "religion," concentrate on this. Read the Bible, especially the Gospel and Epistles (in modern English translations), and do not give up hope. For Christ has said, "Seek and you shall find; knock and it will be opened" (Matthew 7:7–16). I do not believe there is anyone who is living who cannot be saved. With God, all things are possible. God made you and put you here. You are his child. He has not given up on you. He gave you free will so that you can decide for yourself to come home to Him. Amen.

Unstuck

So, we all get stuck. We all reach points in life where we do not know which way to go, where we need help, direction. We all get a feeling of despair or hopelessness. We all sometimes feel depressed or alienated. Why? The answer is that we lose sight of who we are, why we are here, and who is the Master[13] of the universe.[14]

The truth is that there is a reality beyond that which we can see with our eyes of flesh. It is just as real; it is just that one must become aware of it a different way. *We are spirit.* We are children of light. The flesh we think we *are* is really just a house or a vehicle. Just as some people identify with their house or their car, nearly all of us identify with our bodies. We pay much more attention to the body than to anything else—making it healthy, making it look good, making it feel good. Yes, we must take care of it, but really, it is not "ours." It is borrowed. God lent it to us for a purpose: to serve Him and to grow our spirits for His Kingdom. But so often, people do not see this fact. They do not spend much time trying to seek God's purposes for their existence and how they uniquely fit into them. Many Christians are being spoon-fed human ideas about what God wants and not hearing Yahweh himself.

---

[13] In part 2, I explain who He is and why we must acknowledge that, and also why His existence is irrefutable.

[14] I recently had this experience during two surgeries and nine days in the hospital, three emergency visits and a lot of physical pain. My mind was clouded so I couldn't really read the Bible or pray very well. But I was able to focus through some old Gospel music I like and accept the love and care of others—as God sent His angels to lift me up. It was God's hand that led me out of that abyss and brought me back to life. Thus, my balance was restored as I realized He had brought me through as only He can do. Praise Him!

Yahweh sent Jesus Christ into the world and one of His reasons was to show us, His foolish children, how to listen to Him to discern what God intends us to do or to be in this world.

First, we must realize that everything we see including the physical body is very temporary. None of it is expected to last. The world I grew up in—the USA of the 1950s—is as gone as the Roman Empire. That is not to say that I cannot live in this version; I seem to be doing just fine. In the 1950s and 60s, there was very little on TV; and further, although sometimes I made phone calls, most socializing and just about all other human interaction happened in person. It was taken for granted that most people cared about one another. Now we talk online ("online" wasn't even a word when I was young), and shaking hands is almost a lost art. But even though the world has changed, God still reigns as sovereign as ever. So, to be like the early Christians requires adaptation, but it does not require compromise!

We are not meant to focus on ourselves all the time, to center one's focus too much on oneself is idolatry. Raising oneself to some lofty position in one's own mind is pride and is sin (Romans 12:3). In the past, I have focused on my body, my money, my job, given them huge power over my life. I used to worry that if I retired, I might outlive my money! I and most other cancer patients would be happy to outlive our money, but even longevity is not the be-all or the end-all. *Service, humility,* and *grace*, through faith, are of far greater importance.

What we focus on, we empower in our lives. What we empower will determine the direction of the person who empowers it. If we focus too much on the body, we may get it big and strong and beautiful, for a while, but eventually, we will be sorrowful and depressed as it starts to deteriorate with time. I focused on my job to the extent that it became who I was. And because of this, I was a nervous wreck, always worried about losing my position or failing to do well, unable to cope with many of the stresses of daily living. When things didn't go as I had hoped, I became depressed. Others I knew killed themselves. I know how they felt.

So, our first prescription for the *perception* of being stuck is to realize and accept that what is truly valuable, lasting, and worthy is Jesus Christ and to focus our limited attention on Him. Every day, in all we do, more and more. Realize, "I am a spirit, and my function is to serve the Lord, not myself." Eventually, this thought becomes automatic, but we must work on it. If we belong to Him, He should, over time, take up more and more of our attention, leaving less opportunity for the devil to mess with us through negative thoughts, and He will show us a path to be *useful* and to help *other people,* and we will receive many blessings and rewards in the spirit. At least, that is how it has been for me. I could be depressed and unhappy all the time over cancer and all that would happen to my body in the future. Focusing on Jesus is much more rewarding here and now. Focusing on helping people makes my life beautiful and joyful as I also serve God. I don't need selfies in front of the Eiffel Tower. I need real people whose lives I can brighten with simple acts of kindness.

The second prescription is to realize and accept that Yahweh, Creator of Heaven and Earth, put me here for His purpose—that is, to play a part in His plan. My plans, my ideas, are not important. His plan is all-important. I have to focus on understanding His plan as it is revealed to me and on doing His will. So, in the larger picture, if my ideas about my future are swept aside by life events, as is often the case, that says to me that His plan is different and I must try to see what I can do for Him and for fellowman from the new place where He has put me. I have to roll with it. The full plan is not revealed all the time, so we must learn to trust Him. The tempest tosses us all around. Christ is the solid rock.

I was discussing this the other night with one of our guests at the shelter, who is saved and devout, and he fully agrees. He may be temporarily homeless, but he knows he is there to serve the Lord, and this is his focus. It was a blessing to converse with him and see that he and I are on the same page in just about every way.

As a corollary, because no one knows His whole plan, or my part in it, I have to listen to Him. This means, in prayer, I daily seek His advice and follow His directives no matter where they take me. If need be, I will sacrifice my ideas and count it a blessing to be sacrificed for Him. Because Christ, my Lord, sacrificed Himself for me. But also, in my experience, this has led to many unexpected blessings, and this can be true for you also.

Okay, I have cancer. I did my worrying, cried my tears, prayed my terrified prayers, searched frantically for a cure, experienced denial and all the things we must experience because we are human and cannot help it. But when I wound up on my knees at the foot of the cross and received peace in my heart, it dawned on me that I was still alive. My life isn't over until it's over. And that is not today. Therefore, there is a way to still be useful. I just must let Him show me. And so, I have been for these previous three years deeply and personally involved with the homeless in our community. I am sure there will be a call for you too; all you have to do is listen and follow, and the rewards and blessings that flow will be beyond our wildest imaginations. I have cancer, but I would not trade the last three years for anything. My cup runs over with peace and joy in the Holy Spirit. I had to give up dreams and plans, but better things awaited me here.

For those who are still seeking him, does temptation necessarily end with belief and baptism? No! Does sin? No! But the recognition that one's life is on the wrong track can be the start of a transformational journey. If, at some point, one comes to see the flaws and pitfalls of his or her life and how they lead to unhappiness and the feeling of being "stuck," it is not the end; it *could* be the beginning! At some point, we all despair. I am also struggling with these feelings, because just when I felt I had it all worked out, I developed a second form of cancer, as if the first weren't enough—another challenge to remind me we are all human.

As our beloved Paul, Apostle of Christ to all, explains in Romans, those who still have this physical body still have desires and wants. The flesh does one thing from birth to the grave: it *wants*. It wants food, warmth, air, water, and also anything that feels good at the moment—that is, anything that releases the brain's feel-good chemicals.

Now, the mind is different, as Paul points out in Romans 7:7–25. This is our struggle who have been made servants of Christ (i.e., all who have been saved yet have a physical body in which to dwell). Part of it is this: before we met Christ Jesus and had our "road to Damascus" moment, the mind was set on the world—that is, everything was seen from a worldly perspective, it being the only point of view we had.

Ours is not an easy path to follow. The result, however, is release from the prison of the past. Everything that happened in the past has led us to the places we are today—able to hear God, able to follow Christ,

Just waiting for Him to tell us what to do, to serve Him, to serve our fellow man.

Being stuck is a little like being the paralytic who was lowered through a hole in the roof to Christ. He was helpless, and the house was full, and the poor man could not get close enough to receive a healing touch, so his friends lowered him through the roof, and Jesus forgave him and healed him. We just need to hear him say, "Take up your bed and walk," and we will go our way, praising Him (Mark 2:1–12). But He is here with the healing touch for each and every one of us. We just have to believe.

I am neither a preacher nor a psychologist, but I can see that the chains that hold people prisoner are called "the past" and "the future." We ruminate and torture ourselves about the past, about what might have been, about loves lost, the fortunes never made, the pot of gold at the end of a rainbow never pursued . And about our mistakes and bad choices, none of which we can usually do much about now, but even still, we get depressed and think our life is ruined or wasted. But real life isn't in the past; it is in the present. The real life we could be having *today* is what we sacrifice by dwelling in the past.

We also worry about plans and ideas for the future that mostly never come to pass, at least not in the way we imagine. And we fret about misfortunes that might befall us, money we might lose, conditions of the body that might arise, loss of our jobs, loss of our homes, the fate of our children. And somewhere in the back of our mind, our mother or father or brother is laughing, saying, "I told you so." Or we worry that our sins are unforgivable. We worry that dire consequences might arise if we fail at one thing or another. We see negative pictures of our imagined futures in our minds. These pictures are not reality, and the real future rarely matches them. Thus, there is no benefit in dwelling on them. Again, if we spend our energy and focus worrying about the future, we sacrifice the reality of today, giving up the chance of a meaningful present.

I was told by Christ in my vision that He died to take away the past and relieve me of the burdens I carried. [15] I was shown by the Holy

---

[15] See appendix II.

Spirit that I do not need to worry about condemnation or judgment in the future. Amen.

It's not perfect! We still live in a broken world. We are broken people, just like everyone else. Today, I had a fight with my dearly beloved. Bone of my bones and flesh of my flesh. These arguments are not as common as they used to be, nor as ugly, but there was hurt on both sides. Christ and Paul admonish us against anger. Anger shuts down reason and spiritual sight and our pipeline to God through the Holy Spirit. We have to forgive and try to do better in the future. The reason is that the true path is a process; salvation is only the beginning. We have many bumps in the road. But we have Christ to intercede for us, and He understands because He is the Son of Man, fully human as well as divine.

I am still human. I start to worry over "my" plans—to serve the homeless, to be part of the project establishing a permanent shelter for them, to write a second book. How is it possible with two cancers, possibly involving chemotherapy, to accomplish all I imagine in the future?[16] Why did God allow me to have a second form of cancer? Why won't He take it away? Why can't I keep my body as it is until I die, fully functional? It's just not fair.

But I know I am part of *His* plan, and these things are too. And I don't know that He will not arrange all these things a certain way to assist me. I know none of what I do is me. It is Him working through me. And I know my pride must be crushed out of me in His winepress. I need to be humble in His sight. So, if I cannot humble myself, He will make me humble.[17] Amen.

But more than this I recognize that that my thoughts of what "might have been" and "if only" and the "unfairness" of my past are all distractions of the devil, and I simply do not allow them. They are not good for anything. And I ask the Holy Spirit to come and fill me up and leave no room for the devil. And I submit my future to Yahweh.

---

[16] When we think about the future, we see pictures in our head. These are usually just constructs of the mind. Very few are sent by God. We must not become attached to them. They rarely come to pass as we imagine. Nor need we be afraid of them, for the same reason. Things I imagine, like being sick and dying alone, are unlikely to come to pass in that form. They are mere possibilities. I would be foolish to focus on them and empower them in my life.

[17] After I wrote that paragraph, I had nine very humbling days in the hospital.

Sometimes, that is very painful. More than once, I have spent my prayer time weeping over dreams I had and laying them at the foot of the cross, saying goodbye to mental constructs I have loved.

However, my blessing is that I can (after I finish feeling sorry for myself) live for today most of the time, to do His calling. This week, I also had to ask for prayer support from my friends. This is another thing I have found: when it gets hard, they are there to help me focus on God's message and tasks. My tears dry up, and I walk my walk.

What I am trying to say is that there is a life, not just in the future but *here* and *now*, in the flesh, where we do not have to be stuck. Or, if we should find ourselves stuck, there is a prescription to be unstuck for the Christian. Christians (meaning the saved) are not bulletproof. All kinds of things happen to us. Some of us still fall into sin; some still become alcoholics and addicts. Life is hard. But if we hold to Christ, we can find a way out, a way to get unstuck. And Christ, through the Holy Spirit, will help us.

We are also not cancer-proof. Many people online have told me if I just prayed harder and trusted more or had greater faith, God would cure my cancer—or both cancers. However, this statement is misguided. The choice to cure my cancer is not mine; it is God's. He has His reasons and His plans. Some of them are revealed, and some are not. In my case, I think God used cancer to get my attention to save me. I'm not saying He gave me cancer, but He does use things, takes the things that are wrong and terrible, and turns them to good in the end.

Further, life in the flesh is temporary. The body of flesh *has to* die. I have had other people tell me, "No, we will simply go straight to heaven in the Rapture." Now, I do not doubt anything in the Bible, but I have known many good people who were saved Christians who have died, as did Peter, Paul, and the greatest saints of the original Church. Are we greater than they were? And while it is true that there have been instances of people being raised from the dead or miraculously cured, these things are done, not for the sake of the healer or the healed but to show the power of God. For God does have the power to raise the dead, heal the sick and the lame, give sight to the blind, and do all the other things stated in the Bible. And these are done so that people, being weak and fallible as we are, could believe and grow fruitfully.

In my case, as I told in *I, Witness*, I was a content retired person, with things "all worked out." We had enough savings to live comfortably. My two grown sons had found career paths. As soon as my wife retired, we planned to go on some cool vacations, see some interesting places. But five years ago, things started to go south. From an elevated PSA test to a positive biopsy to surgery, radiation, and a stage-4 diagnosis in a matter of months. What to do? Pray, go to church, hope for some advanced immunotherapy. None of it relieved the anxious feelings in my gut. Nor, to be honest, did it help much with my guilt. I put on as brave a face as I could, but inside, I was weak.

Nevertheless, Jesus Christ does come to us and saves—not necessarily the body, but the spirit, and the spirit is more important than the body because the body is meant to be temporary and the spirit is meant to be eternal. Therefore, we should not focus on the body, on the cancer, or whatever malady we might have. We should focus on the spirit and on Jesus Christ and His power to save the spirit. For, in the end, the spirit is what counts. The flesh counts for nothing.

So, if we focus on the Lord, we spend our energy on helping others. We use this body that we have been given freely, until we use it up. We use all of it. We will not leave any of it unused but use it all for the Lord and for other people. Like a champion athlete, we leave it all on the field. I will not save anything or hold back anything, recognizing that the body is a tool, a vehicle, meant to be used, not to be preserved.[18]

In focusing myself this way, I do not empower my feelings of inadequacy, of failure, of depression, guilt, or anxiety; I empower the Holy Spirit, acting through me, and I receive the blessings which accompany that spirit and feel the presence of the spirit. I especially work on not focusing any attention on images about things that might

---

[18] It's not wrong to pursue fitness or education or practice; but these are best thought of as akin to "sharpening God's tools"—not as "*our* accomplishments," a mindset which leads to pride. Whatever knowledge and skills we acquire in this world should be for His glory, not our own. Veneration of individuals for accomplishments is just another form of idolatry and leads to celebrity worship and other destructive things. It is a trap for bad thinking. Everyone is just a sinner, and a frail human being, no matter what they do, and no one can boast in God's presence. So, we should be aware that awards and "accomplishments" should not be taken seriously; if we acquire abilities and use them for Godly work, it is enough.

happen in the future, empowering fear. Empowered, fear can create a kind of paralysis. In centering my focus on Jesus and on helping others, there is no need to "get anywhere"—I am already where I am supposed to be. There is no reason to be afraid. It is simply my choice to *serve* the Lord and fellow man.

God's Rest

I saw something else unfold one day as I read Hebrews chapters 3 and 4. It is so critical that we spend significant time, daily if possible, or at least weekly, alone with Him. "Today, if you hear his voice, do not harden your heart" (Hebrews 4:7). This is so critical because if you are not listening, how do you know what He wants? I prayed every day but only to ask for what *I* wanted. God knows my needs. I said, "Thy will be done," but didn't wait to hear what that will was for my life. I was weak, childish, self-absorbed, and worldly. It is why I so desperately needed saving.

But then Jesus showed me the way to a reconciliation that was life-changing. Now I listen and hear and see and I am willing to be obedient, to do what He wants as well as I can understand it. He sent me to the homeless shelter, where I found an emotional and spiritual home unlike anything I had ever known, a rejuvenating and empowering experience. I received a chance to interact as a new creation in Christ. They didn't know me and didn't ask questions. It was liberating.

When we get a calling in silent prayer, often, we think we are not up to the task, or so it went with me. My friend said, "God doesn't call the qualified; he qualifies the called." Then the church gave me an anointing in the name of Yeshua the Messiah (Jesus Christ). I do often pray for strength from the Holy Spirit as well.

So, God has given me blessings and has given me spirits and has protected me to do his will because I have done my best to be obedient. And one of His callings is to share my story and all that is revealed to me in the spirit. I know my time is limited. I started my deep faith journey with cancer, and now, I have two cancers: prostate cancer and multiple myeloma. MM is kind of scary. I am not looking forward to any part of it. It is painful and debilitating, things I hate. But those things, if they happen, will be temporary. We go *through* them. We don't end with them. We cast off the suit of flesh and go on as spirits until He raises us in a new and perfected form. Amen.[19]

So, I am twice blessed. Blessed by having the honor of serving Him now and blessed by the knowledge that Jesus has me for eternity if I hold true.

---

[19] Those who want to know more about the resurrection of the body are encouraged to read 1 Corinthians 15:35–54.

A Changed Heart

This is my story. Yours will likely be different. Each of us is unique.

I had a vision; I believe it was given by God. It was a strong vision, and I explained it fully in *I, Witness*.[20] Briefly, it had three parts: first, I was shown my sins in a powerful series of flashbacks; then, I saw Jesus Christ, and He briefly spoke to me and removed my burden of sin and guilt; then, the Holy Spirit removed the veil or cloud from my spiritual sight and enabled me to understand the Bible as *written* so that everything made sense to me as never before.

I was in tears in my doctor's office because she is a woman of Christ, and I blurted out that I had been a sinner and my life had been changed. She said, "This is real salvation," words I will always treasure, confirming to me that which I had experienced. I was invited to go to a home church hosted by her and her husband, where I confessed my experience in detail and realized that others in the group had also experienced similar things, through the trials and tribulations of this life. In twenty years at the institutional church I had joined, with a membership of 400 souls, I *never* heard any similar story. I had thought that it was strange that God sent dreams and visions in the Bible times but no longer did. However, now I can see that the unspiritual person, not being able to understand them, *suppresses* them—like Scrooge after meeting the ghost of Marley, at first dismissed as a result of indigestion.

---

[20] See appendix II.

One of our home church friends said to me, "You have been given a great gift." I believe spiritual gifts should be shared or paid forward. I came home that night and over forty-eight hours wrote a very rough first draft of what became *I, Witness.*

PART TWO

A Way to Understand the Whole Bible[21]

---

[21] In order to understand and follow this part, you will benefit greatly by keeping your Bible handy; or downloading a Bible app on your phone or computer. Look up and compare the references and read them in context. You might also notice I have not said "the only way." I do not make that claim. I'm writing these pages for regular people, not Ph. D.s, to have **a** way to make sense of this very intricate collection of writings. Nevertheless, I believe everything I have written is well supported in scripture.

Creation and Fall—the Human Condition

The Bible is one story. It is not "plan A and plan B." It is easy to understand if you don't chop it up into a few verses here and there and read them as unrelated aphorisms in support of a homily. This is how I wish I had been taught from the start and the reason I want to write it for people who are groping to understand it.

As in every history, it begins at the beginning, before recorded time or memory. Before there were people. Before everything. And science and the Bible largely agree, although no one knows the date, because no one was around to make note of it. For science tells us that at some point, some mighty force acted to call forth what we call the "universe" out of the void. We know that nothing in nature moves without some force acting on it. The universe is so big that the force or power that moved it had to be extremely powerful, beyond our imaginations. The existence of this force or power was revealed to ancient people who recognized it as intelligent and purposeful and not merely random. We named the "mighty force" who revealed Himself to us "God" or "Yahweh." Perhaps the best name for Him is just "I AM," the self-reference He used speaking to Moses from the burning bush (Exodus 3:14). "In the beginning God [I AM] created the heavens and the earth" (Genesis 1:1).

God created Adam. "Adam" is the Hebrew word for man. Interestingly, *a-dam-a* is the Hebrew word for earth. God created man out of the earth. "Dam" is the Hebrew for blood, and "the life of a creature is in the blood" (Leviticus 17:11).[22]

It is entirely appropriate for us to venerate and worship the power that created the universe. It is not "imaginary," as demonstrated by the fact that we are here. No one in science can tell you what existed before the creation of the universe. But clearly, the Power that moved the universe into being had to have existed *first* before it could create anything.

---

[22] Some translations: "the life of all flesh."

Shame and Guilt—The
Garden of Eden

Originally, Adam and Eve were naked, and they were not ashamed (Genesis 2:25). Shame came about through man's act of eating "the fruit of the tree of the *knowledge*[23] of good and evil"; for, as soon as they ate, they saw they were naked, and they made coverings for themselves out of leaves (Genesis 3:7). The implication is that they did this because they were ashamed. The Bible does not say they felt guilty because of their disobedience; rather, they were ashamed of their being, as are all God's creatures, naked.[24,25] Thus, they hid themselves not for fear of punishment because they had disobeyed; however, Adam said they were afraid *because* they *were naked*! (Genesis 3:10). Look at these three sentences, Genesis 2:25, 3:7, and 3:10. Notice, "were" is a form of the verb "to be." Shame is poisonous to the spirit because it goes to what one *is* rather than to what one *does*. This use of the verb *to be* implies a state of being, not just the lack of clothing. "They *were* naked." One can correct behavior; we can seek atonement and forgiveness, but we cannot on our own change what we *are*. If we are *ashamed* of what we *are*, we are experiencing this inner affliction. I struggled for many years because of shame, which I will talk more about later in this book.

Guilt is a separate issue. As Paul succinctly points out in Romans

---

[23] Knowledge is also the loss of innocence.
[24] There is a lot here one could delve into deeply, but I am keeping this book short so as to make the Gospel more accessible to everyone.
[25] Some translations state that they "were ashamed"; others do not, but their actions are clear. None say they felt guilt.

3:20 and 5:13, we are not guilty of sin until we have a law to tell us we are guilty even though we know good and evil. For through the law, God judges all people guilty, and the purpose is to make all of us aware of sin.

Now we know that whatever the law says, it says to those who are under the law, so that every mouth may be silenced and all the world held accountable to God. Therefore no one will be declared righteous in God's sight by the works of the law; rather through the law we become conscious of our sin. (Romans 3:19–20)

Paul points out that he would not have known the meaning of "covet" but for the law that says "thou shalt not covet" (see Romans 7:7–9). But as soon as he learned the law, he realized that he was guilty, and sin, which had been dormant in him, sprang to life, and he "died." This description in Romans 7 deals with man struggling with sin and guilt.

From my own experience, I can tell you that guilt is a crushing burden. My guilt was so great it would have killed me before Christ appeared to me in a vision and bore my guilt on His cross. He showed me this and told me it is what He died to do. His love for me was so great that He gave himself to spare me. I described this fully in *I, Witness*. In fact, I had carried my burden of guilt for so long that removing it left me feeling light as a feather for months. In the three years since, the awful weight has not returned. And I try my best to avoid sin as much as I can, even though I know I cannot be perfect and that only Jesus can save.

The reason I write these writings is to share this vision with you, the ones who read, to have your eyes opened. (Not the scoffers. I feel sorry for them.) But I know many still carry burdens of guilt and shame, even some of the saved because the devil confuses people and brings up bad memories and old feelings. He uses other people, even friends, to do this. My own mother carried such a burden to her grave. So sad.

Some are ashamed because they struggle with addiction or other illnesses. Some are guilty over the harm they did to others. Some believe the things over which they feel these feelings of shame and of guilt are so great that they cannot be forgiven. This idea that anyone cannot be forgiven is not true! For God, all things are possible!

Even though it defies the logic of human ideas, and we know we stand condemned; if you can cast away your pride, humble yourself and come to Christ on your knees in true repentance, no matter who you are or what you did, you can still be saved! It is only pride that tells you not to do it. "What will I look like to others? What will my friends think?"

Shame played an important part in my life; though I never knew it or recognized it at the time. My father's physical and psychological cruelty, belittling jokes, the bullying of boys when we moved, and I had to start a new school. Those were all taken to heart. I thought there was something wrong with me. I wasn't as strong as other boys, mostly because I had never had the opportunities to engage in physical activity and sports as other boys mostly had. I was asocial because I never had the chance to mix and play with my peers until I started school and missed out on the early childhood socialization that is so important to being comfortable in one's own skin. Naturally, I feared my father, who at times was tyrannical, and my peers, who were way ahead of me in physical and social development. And all this made me so ashamed that I hated to look in the mirror, believing myself to be ugly and poorly made. Later, I was intensely ashamed of my sexuality because no one had ever bothered to explain it to me.

As I said in *I, Witness*, my parents sent us to church. My mother attended on Easter Sunday; and my father, who was a Marxist and who believed religion is the "opiate of the masses," a fraud to keep the "ignorant" in line, never did.

Our first church was an old-fashioned Methodist Church, where the sermons were heavy on sin and damnation. So, I knew early that nearly everything I did in life was sinful, although I never fully understood why. And although I never intended to hurt anyone, I continued to sin.

Abraham

So back to our Biblical timeline, we meet Abram. Abram was a goatherd in the land of Ur (Now Iraq) near the Euphrates, one of the four rivers that bounded the Garden of Eden (see Genesis 12:1). Now, Abram was a person who listened to God, who recognized his voice, who trusted in Him and obeyed. So, whatever God said, He would call "Abram" or "Abraham," and he would answer, "Here I am" (Genesis 22:1; see Acts 7:1–8). Because of his obedience and his belief and his trust in God, God would even come to him at times in human form, just as he did with Adam and Eve in the garden (see Genesis 18 for one example).

And so, when God told him to take all that was his and leave and go to a new place that God would show him, he obeyed (Genesis 12: 1–5). Now, Abram's wife Sarai was barren, and he had no children. God, however, does not just abandon His faithful servants, but rather, even when they were a hundred years old God promised him children, and because he believed God, and God granted him righteousness based on faith (Genesis 15:6, Romans 4:3, Galatians 3:6). This is foundational for our understanding of justification through faith. No one can be perfectly righteous on his own, but God grants His grace to the faithful believers in Christ.

Years later, God called Abraham, and he answered, "Here I am." God told him to take his son Isaac to the place he would show him and sacrifice him (Genesis 22:2). Abraham obeyed, and therefore, he received the promise, which is the foundation of redemptive history (Genesis 22:15–18). For God promised him an heir, which is Christ Jesus (Galatians 3:16). Furthermore, God intervened at the last second to save

Isaac and gave Abraham a *substitute* sacrifice, a ram whose horn was caught in a thicket (Genesis 22:12–14).[26] And the blessing (salvation) is to all the nations of the world, to those who believe in Jesus. And the Land is the Kingdom of Heaven. Paul states clearly that Yeshua (Jesus) is the heir and we hold our portion because we are "clothed" with him (Galatians 3:27).[27]

In Matthew 22:1–15, the parable of the wedding feast, there is one guest who was thrown out because he is not wearing this "clothing" (Matthew 22:11–14; see also Ephesians 4:24). The wedding feast is the eschatological (a $50 word for "end times") wedding of Christ and his people. The wedding is an analogy. We are to form a spiritual union that is unbreakable with Christ. To be united with Him, we first have to ditch the public-school brainwashing that says the physical world is all there is, and the universe is completely random; we *must* believe in God, that which gives order to our existence. This is very difficult or impossible for many people because of the devil's doctrine of materialism, pushed in public school and on television and the public square. Materialism is also the basis of communism and existentialism.

The point is that we must be saved to partake in the eternal reward.[28] *I, Witness* was the story of my personal salvation, how I received the gift in a vision that restored my belief in God, in the Risen Christ. It is all true, and if you believe *in Him*, however it happens, you will also be saved (Romans 10:9, John 6:28–9). If you don't understand or are not sure, I suggest you read it. I am not special; I am a regular person, a sinner just like you, but Christ, by His mercy, did an extraordinary thing to save me. Other people I know have had similar experiences. I post some of their testimonies on my website. Everyone doesn't have visions, and this is not essential to salvation; but if you do, I believe it's important to share them for the benefit of others. There are some who suppress or deny their experiences and others who are just afraid to talk about them.

---

[26] The introduction of a *substitute* sacrifice is a direct portent of the future sacrifice of Jesus Christ, who died in place of all sinners, the Lamb of God.

[27] Everything in the Bible is likely to have multiple meanings. So, the land is also Israel, and the progeny is the Hebrew Nation, and the blessings are also the material and spiritual blessings they enjoyed. But the eternal blessings are also for us, for all nations for all time— the blessings of salvation through Jesus Christ.

[28] That is, to come to a profound belief, submit to Christ and receive the blessing.

Paul explains that the promise of a blessing to the nations[29] was to the Gentiles as well as to the Jews (Romans 4:11–13). The descendants without number in Revelation 7 are all the people everywhere who were later to believe in Christ in the future generations (see Revelation 7:14–17). The blessing is the salvation that the sacrifice bought (Hebrews 9:14–28). But why the blood? Why death? Those are key questions, and ones I think some churches fail to answer clearly or to talk about enough at least.

I will say, by way of preface, that the sacrifice of an animal (or more than one) was not unique to the Hebrews. Pagans also gave blood sacrifices to their stone statues. Furthermore, contracts, promises, and wills (covenants) were also commonly sealed with blood. People recognized from early days that when you open an animal's (or a man's) veins and let out the blood, it dies. The life of the flesh is in the blood. Thus, blood is precious. Significant. Serious. We are also aware that we are culturally different from these people. Most of us in the twenty-first century are not used to blood, intestines, and internal organs. They may think these things are "gross." But these people raised animals for slaughter, and it was their way of life. So, blood and the insides of animals was not "gross"; it was an everyday part of life. If you wanted dinner, you killed an animal, removed its insides, and then cooked it, or you went hungry. So, blood was something they had readily available as well.

Now, is it any wonder that when God wanted these people to take a vow seriously, He demanded blood; and when the people were brought out of the land of Egypt, it was blood that was the seal of safety, the Passover? And being spring, the slaughter of the spring lambs was a natural part of life.

Next, God brought a very large number of people out of Egypt, only half of which were genetic descendants of Abraham. They had no system of laws, courts, or governance; no unifying culture; no codified religion. However, at Mount Sinai, He gave them all these things in one package and made a contract with them that if they would be His people, He would be their God (Exodus 19:1–7). And as people subject to God, they had to obey His rules (Exodus 19:5).

---

[29] Genesis 22:16–18. The use of nations, plural, means it is to everyone who believes regardless of race or background.

The Amazing Book of Hebrews and the New Covenant—The Book That Ties the Whole Bible Together

Reading one day and trying to fathom the traditions of the Hebrews and the sacrificial system, I was dumbstruck at the fantastic explanations and the connections to the Old Testament and the full richness of this amazing portion of the Bible! For example, the ties between the priesthood, Melchizedek in chapter 14 of Genesis, and Christ the High Priest. I realized that this short book, which was originally a letter or sermon, contains a short version explanation of our entire redemptive history, and compact Christian theology, all in one simply written document.

In the Old Testament, God (YHWH) brought His people to Mount Sinai in the desert and gave them their entire culture—religion, government, customs, and laws—in one package with fire and thunder. He essentially created a *new civilization* that had never existed before, unlike any in history. The central features included the Levitical priesthood and a system of feasts and sacrifices in a tabernacle that was a copy of God's throne room in heaven, shown to Moses by God. Hebrews explains how and why the old system is replaced by the New Covenant at the resurrection of Jesus Christ, having fulfilled its function; and that for us, He is the Way, the Truth, and the Life. Further, this was *always* God's plan; it is not "plan B." The Law of Moses was given to create a place and a people to which YHWH would later send His Son, the Messiah, to fulfill His prophesies in the Old Testament and provide a path of salvation to the human race.

Chapter 1 sometimes is glossed over, but I think it is of great importance, establishing that Jesus is the Son of God and was here from the foundation of the world (Hebrews 1:10), just as also stated in John 1:1–4. And He is indeed the Son of God. In chapter 2, the author states that Christ willingly tasted of death, lowering Himself so He would call us mortal people, sharing the experience of suffering and death, His brothers (Hebrews 2:9–13). Further, through *suffering*, He perfected Himself and us so that He and we could be one, sanctified through *suffering* (Hebrews 2:10–12). "So, Jesus is not ashamed to call them brothers and sisters" (Hebrews 2:11). "And again, 'I will put my trust in him.' And again He says, 'Here am I and the children God has given me" (Hebrews 2:13). So, for us who suffer and die, we find here another reason for our pain and all the trials of this life. In pain, in suffering, and even in death, we are *united* with Christ. We are truly His brothers and sisters, having shared these experiences with Him, and He with us, not because He had to—because He loved us that much!

Hebrews 3 emphasizes the need for being saved. Those who hear the word and do not believe cannot enter God's rest. This calls into question the practice of some organizations of allowing the unsaved to be members. This puts the cart before the horse in a most destructive way. For I do not think a person can be a member of the body of Christ (see Romans 12) until he is first saved, and *then*, being first saved, he has to live and learn a Christian life. Being a member of a Church organization, as per human pronouncement and ritual, does not make anyone saved. Otherwise, how would it be different from "the works of the law"?[30] No, salvation is an experience or set of life experiences that a person goes through that changes him; one believes in and surrenders to Christ, and we receive His Spirit in our hearts. Some of these experiences are *necessarily* painful. If anyone sincerely wants this and asks, with a heart to live or die or suffer for the Lord, it will be given (John 5:24). But if you think going through the motions in some ritual or sacrament can give you (or your children) eternal life, that is not how I read the Gospel.

Many people today are deprived of an early opportunity to be saved

---

[30] Paul discusses in detail in Romans 9 and other places that simply following form and tradition and ritual is insufficient to save and we are only saved by grace through faith. It is the Spirit, living in us, that is the sign of salvation.

by being given an adulterated Gospel in church. Like wine mixed with too much water, it is of no effect. They grow up going to church, but many leave when they become adults because the seed that was planted was never given a chance to grow. Or maybe, rather than a weak Gospel, in some cases, it is just that it is pushed at young people who aren't ready to receive it. And it isn't their fault. They get a one-hour lecture on Jesus once a week and live on cartoons and video games the rest. And in between, we have Santa Claus, the Easter Bunny, the Tooth Fairy, and lots of chocolate and toys and things that have nothing to do with the Spirit. Soon they realize that much of what they have been told isn't real. The real is just for the grown-ups. It is hard to overlook this hypocrisy. In saying these things, I cannot claim to be any better. I made the same mistakes.

The winds of life shake and test everyone severely. Blind and groping, we feel our way along because we are still trapped in the tent of flesh. We lose sight of Him and come to Him on our knees again. What can we do? Only persevere in prayer and right action and self-reflection, knowing always that Christ our Lord died to free us and bring the lost sheep to the fold. Many of us are the lost sheep. And He works all the time to save us!

Hebrews 4 contains the essence of the good news in a short, easily understood form for anyone to hear and respond. God's anger toward the people in the desert was for their disobedience and failure to accept the offered covenant, and those who hardened their hearts died in the desert. People don't always accept the Gospel at first. Yet, David spoke of "another day" in Psalm 95. So, today could be your day, if you are still seeking; today, if you hear His voice, do not harden your heart! And, Christ, the High Priest can take your confession, no matter what you have done, or if you are in prison or in a foxhole or dying in hospice. Do not harden your heart. He has already seen everything inside you. Open your heart and let Him in if you have not already done so. Experience the peace and joy and comfort of joining with Him. Those who have already done so, please pray for the seekers.

Beginning at Hebrews 6:13, the author sets forth the theology of the New Testament in a series of explanations in terms of the old covenant and the system of priests and sacrifices in the temple or tabernacle of Moses.[31] To understand the next section, you need to know about Melchizedek, priest of God Most High.

In my personal vision, Yeshua (Jesus) fulfilled the role of priest-confessor. The difference in function between a priest and a pastor or leader is that a priest is one who intercedes for us with YHWH. The same person can at different times be both, but intercession is the exclusively priestly function. Yeshua (Jesus) did not appoint Himself, but was appointed by God Most High, a priest forever in the Order of Melchizedek (Hebrews 5:5–6, Psalms 110:4, Hebrews 7:17). Melchizedek first appears in Genesis 14:17–20. After Abram (who later became Abraham) rescues Lot, his nephew, from invaders, he enters the Valley of Kings.

> Then Melchizedek King of Salem brought out bread and wine. He was priest of God Most High, and he blessed Abram saying, "Blessed be Abram by God Most High, Creator of heaven and earth; And praise be to God Most High, who delivered your enemies into your hand;" Then Abram gave him a tenth of everything. (Genesis 14:17–20, NIV)

There are some interesting things about this. First, there was no established earthly priesthood until God gave the law to Moses *500 years after Abraham died*! Paul (the author of Hebrews) said his name means "king of righteousness," and "King of Salem" means "King of Peace" in Hebrew (Hebrews 7:2). The worldly priests under the law had to be descendants of Aaron and to have a proven genealogy, but Melchizedek had neither; nor birth or death (Hebrews 7:3). The author of Hebrews also points out that we only tithe to one greater than ourselves, yet

---

[31] The sacrifices of animals in the temple, with the hereditary priesthood, the pouring out of blood and the incense and feasts and celebrations were the center of spiritual life for the Hebrews. If one sinned, they had to bring the sacrifice to Jerusalem to the temple. The priests poured out the blood on the altar. There were sin offerings, burnt offerings, peace offerings, etc. And then the festivals for new moons. And of course, Passover and the Day of Atonement. So, these went on continually. They all had to come to Jerusalem three times a year for the spring festivals of Passover and Firstfruits and the fall feasts of Tabernacles and Day of Atonement.

the Patriarch of the Hebrew Nation tithed to Melchizedek (Hebrews 7:7–10). Thus, Melchizedek was not an ordinary earthly priest nor an ordinary worldly king but a Heavenly priest, priest of God Most High! And, Yeshua was appointed Great High Priest by God, after the order of Melchizedek.

The reason we need to know this is so that we can understand how Christ intercedes with God for us. In the Levitical system, the High Priest alone could enter the Holy of Holies, the innermost chamber where the Ark of the Covenant was kept, and only once a year on the day of atonement, and only with blood for his sins and the sins of the people. Other sacrifices were made year-round, save Passover and the day of atonement. But they were done at the altar in the outer courtyard, and no one else could enter the Holy of Holies.

The temple, the priesthood, the feasts, and the blood sacrifices together were the heart and soul of the religious practice of the ancient Hebrews. Every Hebrew had to travel to the temple three times a year, whether it was in Jerusalem, in Bethlehem, or a tent in the desert. They also held celebrations and Sabbaths for all of these events, and additionally for new moons as well as the seventh day of every week. Thus, these practices were *essential* to the Biblical Hebrews. The priests' job included tracking the moon, keeping the calendar, officiating at all these events, and reading the Torah to people assembled on Holy Days, as well as officiating at sacrifices of blood and gathering the blood and pouring it out on the altar, burning what is to be burnt, and all the other details as set out in Leviticus. Yeshua was also the Paschal Lamb, the sin sacrifice, and the blood of atonement for us. In fact, He fulfilled the entire Hebrew law *for* us, so that when His Spirit dwells in us, we have *fulfilled* the law; because we are "clothed" with Him. It is this *Spirit* that imparts to us a righteousness that we have not earned and cannot attain by ourselves.

As in Romans and Galatians, the author reminds us of the promise to Abraham of land, descendants and blessing, secured by God's oath. The promise of blessing goes to the future of Israel but also reaches the distant future and extends to *nations*, plural (Hebrews 6:13–20, Genesis 22:16–18). This means that it includes Gentiles, who are not physical descendants of Abraham but who live in our time and have faith in Jesus (see also Romans 4:9–17). Jesus is the *heir* of this promise, as of a will (Galatians 3:15–20). And we hold our portion through Him (Galatians 3:26–29).

Beginning at Hebrews 7:11, the author makes the logical point that if perfection had been attainable through the Levitical priesthood,[32] there would have been no need for a priest according to the order of Melchizedek. Moreover, in 7:12, he proclaims that when there is a change in the priesthood, there must also be a change in the law. As an example, he points out Yeshua (Jesus) was not descended from Aaron but from Judah! And there is no mention in any of the Torah of any priest coming from that tribe. In Hebrews 7:15–19, he concludes that the earlier commandment has been *abrogated* and replaced by a *better* hope.[33] And further, the better hope is secured by God's oath. The rest, Hebrews 7:23–28 proclaims the superiority of Christ as great high priest over the Levitical priesthood; permanency, perfection, power to save.

In Hebrews 8:1–5, the author states the superiority of "the true tent" in heaven over the worldly tent or tabernacle of Moses. In 8:6–7 he states the new covenant is a better ministry, a better covenant, and enacted through better promises (salvation, eternal life, the Holy Spirit). In Hebrews 8:8–12, he quotes Jeremiah 31:27–33 on the new covenant. He emphasizes that Jeremiah recorded God's promise of a new covenant that would not be like the old covenant. He sets forth the entire quote twice, emphasizing its significance. He states openly, "In speaking of a new covenant he has made the old one obsolete." He concludes prophetically, "and, what is obsolete and growing old will soon disappear" (Hebrews 8:13).

This turned out to be prophetic in the physical world as well because a few years later, in AD 70, the Roman legion completely destroyed the Second Temple. The Levitical priesthood, having no place to be consecrated, disappeared. The sacrifices, having nowhere to be offered, ceased. In 2,000 years, this has been unchanged. The worldly system of blood sacrifices, of bulls and rams—has ended.

---

[32] "Levitical" because it is established in the Book of Leviticus.

[33] In the Torah, as they saw it there were not just ten Commandments, but everything in the Torah was a commandment from God; all were mandatory and essential to their religion.

A strong theme emerges. The old is at an end; the new has replaced it. And if we look at 2 Corinthians 3:4–18, the "fading glory" of Moses adds to that theme as well. Galatians 3, Colossians 2, and Romans 3–4 also add weight to this argument. We might also consider Acts 11 and especially Acts 15 as conclusive evidence that the law of Moses no longer binds the Christian. Also see Galatians 3:23–26. This is why Paul states that if one is led by the Spirit, he is not under the law (Romans 7:1–6; Galatians 5:18; there are many more places that could be cited; if you read the New Testament you can easily find them).[34]

Nothing could be clearer. The old is fading away. God has come forth with the new. There is no other reasonable interpretation of all these Scriptures. And it is not just Paul. It is the entire New Testament, and also the prophets, like Jeremiah 31:27–34. This is the reason believers in the New Covenant are on solid Biblical footing.

And the scripture clearly states *why* the New Covenant is superior to the old. As stated previously, in ancient times, only on one day per year, the high priest alone entered the holy of holies, with the blood he offers for himself and for the people for sins unintentionally committed. Paul states,

> This is an illustration for the present time, indicating that the gifts and sacrifices being offered were not able to clear the conscience of the worshiper. They are only a matter of food and drink and various ceremonial washings—external regulations applying until the time of the new order. (Hebrews 9:9–10)

In Hebrews 9:11–14, Paul (the author) says clearly again,

> But when Christ came as high priest of the good things that are now already here, he went through the greater and more perfect tabernacle that was not made by

---

[34] It would be good to stop and read these passages in Biblical context at this point. This is an area that may be debated by some folks. You need to be sure I did not make any of this up. It is in the Bible in black and white. This is also one place where it helps to have a Bible written in modern English, so you can follow the logic more easily.

human hands, that is to say is not a part of this creation. He did not enter by means of the blood of goats and calves; but he entered the Most Holy Place once for all by his own blood, thus obtaining eternal redemption. (Hebrews 9:11–12)

[The ritual sacrifices of the Hebrews] ... Sprinkled on those who are ceremonially unclean sanctify them so that they are outwardly clean. How much more then will the blood of Christ, who through the eternal Spirit offered himself unblemished to God cleanse the consciences from acts that lead to death, so that we may serve the living God! (Hebrews 9:13–14)

Powerful! This is salvation—purification from sin by the blood of Christ Jesus through a deep and profound faith. And with this, we who believe in Him are promised eternal life and resurrection.

In Hebrews 9:15, Paul again emphasizes that Jesus is the mediator of a *new* covenant; for a death has occurred that paid for the transgressions committed under the old covenant. He analogizes this to a will (see also Galatians 3:15–18). A will takes effect upon a death, and he goes on to explain that even under the old covenant, nothing is made clean without blood, invoking the image of Moses sprinkling blood mixed with water, using hyssop and scarlet wool, on the people and on the tabernacle. He continues to say these were only *sketches* of what was to come, the tent, a mere copy of the true tent—but Christ now has appeared in heaven, in the presence of God. Christ, having died once for sins, will appear again, not as a sacrifice but to claim those who are eagerly waiting for him (Hebrews 9:28). In Hebrews 10, the author expounds the point by asking a question: If the sacrifices of animals had been effective to take away sin, would they not have cleared men's consciences by doing them once rather than having to be repeated year after year? (See Hebrews 10:11–18). The repetition is a reminder of sin. Mark 1 begs this question as well, as will be explained later.

Day after day every priest stands and performs his religious duties; again and again he offers the same sacrifices, which can never take away sins. But when this priest had offered for all time one sacrifice for sins, he sat down at the right hand of God, and since that time he waits for his enemies to be made his footstool. For by one sacrifice, he has made perfect forever those who are being made holy. (Hebrews 10:11–14)

Again, the author quotes Jeremiah 31, emphasizing where there is truly forgiveness no further offering is needed, for God will no longer remember our past sins! (Hebrews 10:19–21)

You can see from this how the whole Bible fits and is all one story. I am not the first person to say this. It is right there in black and white (read Ephesians 1:3–14). God's plan has been set in place "from the foundations of the world," and Christ is the cornerstone (Ephesians 2:20). But now, because we have a better promise and a better ministry, God has abolished the law with its commandments and ordinances (Ephesians 2:15). We who believe are led by Christ and no longer need all these rules and rituals (see Romans 13:5–10, Galatians 5:22–26).

And it is also obvious to me that since an all-knowing God created man with intellect, capable of understanding who God is and making a personal choice to worship and obey God, that is what He wants us to do *voluntarily*. A choice is not a choice unless it is voluntary. If you look at Acts 17:26–28, it says precisely the same thing. God wants us to search for Him and find Him, "though he is not far from any one of us" (Acts 17:27). But from the beginning, He foreknew that not all of us would. And so, He planned to send His Son into our midst to give everyone a second opportunity in this fallen, sinful world. And those who follow Him will never be put to shame (Romans 9:33).

Additionally, the purpose of the Hebrew law was to prepare the place and the people for Jesus to come into the world. It was to separate God's people from others, to teach them and prepare them to receive Him. He was not to be born to just any person, or just any place—He is special and had to come to a special place unlike any other place.

We who open our hearts to Him receive the Holy Spirit are clothed in a righteousness we cannot attain any other way. We do not earn it. We do not deserve it. We receive it like a baby receives mother's milk. The Spirit dwells in us, and Christ clothes us (see John 10:7–10, 14–18, 27–30; Galatians 3:26–29; Ephesians 2:1–10. Reading these passages in context and praying on them will give you deeper insight into these things.)

Why It's Important to Us in the Twenty-First Century

We live in a culture of materialism and nihilism and weak religion. I say that while realizing it is not descriptive of everyone. To those who are living in the Lord and have the Holy Spirit, I apologize. But I will say this: there is no "salvation by works." No matter how many "good deeds" you do, no matter what church you go to or what rituals you perform, if you are not saved and have not received the Holy Spirit, it will avail you nothing unless you combine it with faith in Jesus (Hebrews 4:1–3). But there is hope! Hope for you, hope for me, hope for everyone. Yeshua (Jesus), the Great High Priest, is waiting to clear your sins and you can get to Him, 24/7/365.

Also, there are many Christian believers nowadays who are rediscovering the roots in the Old Testament, a positive trend because Yeshua said, "Salvation is from the Jews" (John 4:22). However, many may be going too far, even following dietary prohibitions and new moons, and other ancient rituals as if these "works of the law" could in any way produce salvation. I fear a revival of the "Judaizers" Paul opposed in Acts 15 and in Galatians. They would view every New Testament precept as a mere polishing of the Torah. This is false. The New Covenant is Biblical (see, e.g., Jeremiah 31:27–33; 2 Corinthians 3; Hebrews chapters 8–12); and it exceeds the old as much as a jet fighter exceeds a horse (read 2 Corinthians 3:7–18 if you don't believe it). "For what was glorious has no glory now in comparison with the surpassing glory" (2 Corinthians 3:10).

We, who have accepted Jesus Christ, are raised up to be children of light, i.e. spiritual beings, and we need to understand that, because we are in a spiritual war with dark and mysterious powers (Ephesians 6:10–12) that are invisible to the unspiritual and the spiritually blind. But we have a miraculous "superpower" in the Holy Spirit to help us and see us through, if we understand that and let it work in us.

On the other hand, I think some go too far the other way, holding the view that the Old Testament is just an obsolete vessel having no significance for the Christian. I think this goes way too far. Yes, Yeshua came to save us by His blood. Yes, the work was done on the cross. Yes, we are saved by grace through faith. And the greatest commandment is to love the Lord with all your heart, all your strength, and all your mind. And yes, love your neighbor as yourself. But this is not the entire story. A person in a communist prison under torture to renounce Christ or a person suffering incurable illness, or one afflicted with a disease of the spirit that makes him want to take his own life, needs more. Grounding in the Old Testament is necessary for a greater understanding of the New. And understanding deepens the faith and strengthens our ability to withstand challenges. It gives us ways to call on the Holy Spirit. It also allows one to counter silly arguments, by the enemies of faith, one encounters continually on Facebook and elsewhere in modern society. While people can be saved without knowing much or even without having ever seen a Bible, the full knowledge helps protect a person from being led astray, intimidated, or suffered any other evils the devil has thrown at him. Remember, it is not we who win the fight; it is God through, the Holy Spirit. Knowledge just gives us an edge to call on the power of God to help us when we need it.

In this modern world, many people struggle with the concept of Spirit.[35] It is hard for them to believe. Yet they can easily believe a talking head in a science video on YouTube talking about "dark matter" or events billions of years in the future, as if they were facts. Why? We have been brainwashed! Materialism is more than the quest for cars and clothes and houses and cash. It is also a belief, a religion that says the material world is all there is. That is why Karl Marx called his

---

[35] The author's experience is described in detail in *I, Witness* (Christian Faith Publishing, 2020).

philosophy *dialectical materialism*. He thought if the material world is all there is, then it is up to us to build the world we want to live in, and since we are all there is, there is no one to stop us but ourselves. And the "ends" (good intentions) justify the "means"—lies, violence, intimidation, oppression, destruction, confiscation of property, and murder. No God, no rules.

I believe the answer is simple, and it is offered in plain language right in the Bible, in terms that are clear and unambiguous. If you read the Bible with fresh eyes and believe it actually means what it says, it is right in front of you. This does not necessarily mean literalism. There are things in the Bible that are obviously allegorical, that are obvious intentional overstatements, mere figures of speech. They are not "wrong"; they are just stated in a certain literary style, just as they are in many other books. Why it isn't usually taught that way is another discussion. I say it is partly because the teachers are blinded by the devil. But after reading John 9 and learning about spiritual sight, you can decide for yourself.

John 9: Spiritual Blindness and the Gift of Sight—How Spirit Is the Key to Understanding

One day, as I was reading, I was just amazed at an interplay of themes and revelations in this one passage. How could I have missed before seeing the rich tapestry as the parts wove together and formed a fantastic mandala of themes and revelations? Reading back over it, even more things jumped off the page. It was so rich, I needed to write it down and record it.

The point of this section is that Christ can also teach us to become spiritual and to "see" with spiritual eyes things that the worldly people cannot see, thus vastly enriching our lives. Only by learning through the Holy Spirit to see with spiritual sight can we come to His deeper understandings. Also, in life, this allows us to "see" the spirits of other people in ways we have not previously, to love the unlovable, to understand the things the world rejects.

The story has levels like layers of an onion. It opens at a time when Jesus is engaged in spiritual contention with the Pharisees, who have identified Him as a threat to their positions and teachings. They are actually following Him around, trying to trick Him and discredit Him in the eyes of the people, unsuccessfully, of course. And they are frustrated and angry and want Him gone.

This has been especially true in the preceding chapters, John 6, 7, and 8. Two themes pertinent to the discussion stand out clearly in all of John's Gospel: *sight* and *spirit*. As we will see, the Pharisees and priests of the temple have little of either at this time. They have become prideful and worldly, forgetting that they are servants of God and of the people.

Things start to really heat up when Jesus goes to the feast of tabernacles.[36] At John 7:14–15, Jesus teaches,[37] and the Jews were amazed at His wisdom, not knowing how He acquired it.[38] In John 7:19, Jesus accuses the Pharisees of failing to keep the law. The Pharisees were experts in the law. But they were also experts at using the law to their own benefit.

One example is found in Mark, chapter 7.

> And He continued, "you have a fine way of setting aside the commands of God in order to observe your own traditions! For Moses said 'honor your father and your mother,' and 'anyone who curses their father or mother is to be put to death.' But you say that if anyone declares that what might have been used to help their father or mother is Corban (that is, devoted to God)-- then you no longer let them do anything for their father or mother. Thus, you nullify the word of God by your tradition which you have handed down. And you do many things like that." (Mark 7:9–13)

In other words, the Pharisees and the priests were robbing the old people for their own benefit. A person would pledge his excess earnings to the temple, and thereafter, the priests would not allow him to help his elderly parents.

Look at Isaiah 1:11–22. God is not interested in people performing rituals and feasts and sacrifices who neglect the poor, the elderly, the widows, the orphans, and other people within their own society who need help. God always expected His people to take care of one another.

---

[36] This was one of the original feasts of the Hebrew religion, given them by God to remember the time in the desert. A tabernacle is a tent.

[37] Circumcised Hebrews were allowed to teach in the temple, although it was risky if the Pharisees didn't like what he had to say.

[38] Generally, when it talks about "the Jews" in John's gospel, it refers to the Priests and the teachers, not the common people, most of whom are impressed by Jesus, and are amazed at the miracles He does, and seek His blessing and power to heal.

The Pharisees were criticizing Him over the healing at the pool in John 5:1–15. This was on the Sabbath. Jesus responds, "Now if a boy can be circumcised on the Sabbath that the law of Moses not be broken, why are you angry with me for healing a man's whole body on the Sabbath? Stop judging by mere appearances, but instead judge correctly" (John 7:23–24). Boy babies had to be circumcised on the eighth day,[39] even if it was the Sabbath. Yeshua also points out that circumcision was not from Moses but from the patriarchs (500 years before Moses). The priesthood was established by the law of Moses, and this remark was bound to irritate them. Circumcision was the hallmark of being a Jew. It was death for an uncircumcised person to enter the inner temple. One could enter past the outer courtyard only if he were circumcised.

Why was Jesus always healing people on the Sabbath? That was the day all the people congregated to hear the reading of the Torah and offer sacrifices. The rest of the week was nonstop toil in fields and pastures and whatever else they did for a living. Jesus did not come to talk only to the priests and Pharisees, so he did most of His work on the Sabbath when the common people were gathered so that everyone could see the power of God and hear the good news that the kingdom of God was near.

The Pharisees and priests were being rigid, legalistic. They were insisting on strict adherence to the letter and ritualistic practice, not looking to the spirit behind the letter. This is why they could not make a "correct" judgment. Yeshua knew the Father and knew His spirit. "'Whoever believes in me, as the scripture has said, rivers of living water will flow from within him.' By this He meant the spirit, whom those who believed in Him were later to receive" (John 7:37–39). Again, He focuses us on a spiritual reality that transcends worldly appearances.

What is the importance of this? They did not acknowledge Yeshua as the Messiah. They knew the prophesies about the Messiah but did not see that He fulfilled all of them. This was partly because they were

---

[39] Numbers were very important to the Hebrews of ancient times. Seven signified completion, three and multiples of three signified importance, and one, new beginnings. The "eighth day" gives the parents the first week to prepare, recover, and come to Jerusalem to the temple with their offering, and is the first day of the second week of life, signifying a new beginning.

hung up on a verse that says, "No prophet shall come out of Galilee" (see John 7:45–52). They were not thinking He could have had different origins. They assumed they knew who He was. Again, they show they are blind to the truth and grace of the Lord. They knew the words but not the living Spirit.

Yeshua said, "I am the light of the world" (John 8:12). This is key. Yeshua is the spiritual light; He brings the knowing of spirit and truth. He brings the genuine sight. Those who only see with the eye are blind. Again, He declares "You do not know me or my Father" (John 8:19, speaking to the priests in the temple).

The contest really heats up in John 8:42–47, where Yeshua accuses the priests of being children of the devil. Yeshua has declared Himself; and He has condemned the priests of the temple for their closed eyes and ears and blindness, which He is soon to demonstrate. He proclaims the Good News in clear terms. "I tell you truly whoever obeys my word will never see death" (John 8:51). This is the Gospel in a nutshell. The priests and the Pharisees reject it. "Are you greater than our father Abraham?" (John 8:53). Christ declares His divinity ("Before Abraham was born, I am!"[40], and they pick up stones to kill Him, but He slips away (John 8:58–9). This then sets the stage for what Christ does next.

---

[40] I AM was how God referred to Himself speaking to Moses from the burning bush, remember? The Jews knew this scripture and that Jesus was placing Himself equal to God—blasphemy in their eyes (see also John 1:1–4).

The Man Born Blind

As the story begins, Yeshua (Jesus; Iesus) comes upon a man born blind, a beggar, and His disciples question, "Rabbi, who sinned, this man or his parents, that he was born blind?" (John 9:2). This is because in the culture of that time, physical affliction, and disability were often considered to be direct punishments of specific sins rather than simply the results of living in a broken world. However, Yeshua responds that neither sinned, but rather, this was to demonstrate God's sovereignty and power over all things. Further, Yeshua is the light of the world, but darkness is coming, so God's work must be done while there is light. (And by analogy, we must do God's work while we may, as our lives in this tent of flesh are short.)

Yeshua makes mud out of dust and spittle (technically, "work") and puts it on the eyes of the blind man—on the Sabbath, thus breaking the Pharisees' strict ritualistic rules of the Sabbath (John 9:6). Do we believe this was coincidental or intentional? Obviously, it was intentional. The Messiah wanted to directly challenge the priests and the Pharisees, the experts in the law. Yeshua sends the blind man to wash in the pool called *Siloam*, meaning "sent."[41] We will see that he is truly sent as we peel the layers of the story (John 9:7).

The man, having been given sight, returned home, and those who knew him were amazed. They questioned whether he could be the same man who was born blind, but he assured them that he was. He testified

---

[41] It is interesting, that there is a difference in the Bible between "called" and "sent." While it is not 100 percent consistent, usually people are called to service or to duty. Most of the time, people are *sent* to speak truth to power, as Moses was sent to Pharaoh.

that he was healed by the one called Yeshua (or Jesus)[42] (John 9:9–11). They took him to the synagogue to be examined by the priests and the Pharisees (John 9:12).

The priests and the Pharisees question the blind man who now sees. Their concern is that Yeshua performed "work" on the Sabbath, a clear violation of the rules and regulations of the Sabbath day. In their legalistic minds, no true man of God would do such a thing. But others said that only a man of God could perform this miraculous sign (John 9:13–16). Therefore, they asked the formerly blind man his opinion, and he replied, "He is a prophet" (John 9:17). This simple truth spoken by the man born blind indicates a simple and straightforward understanding that the person who had given him sight was empowered by God. Having no reason to lie, he simply states the truth.

Now the authorities, fearing the influence of Yeshua, had previously agreed that anyone who said Yeshua was the Messiah should be expelled from the synagogue (John 9:22). This was a dire punishment because it meant ostracism from the community and from the faith, essentially becoming "unclean." They would be banned from association.

Under this threat, they questioned the man's parents, who admitted he was their son and that he had been born blind but disclaimed all knowledge of his cure, saying, "Ask him. He is of age, he will speak for himself" (John 9:21). This was because they feared being put out of the synagogue (John 9:20–21). The parents of the man born blind were afraid of the punishment of the Pharisees and the priests in the temple. They knew that they could be expelled and ostracized and that this would have severe consequences in their lives. Therefore, they took an easy way out.

So, the Pharisees questioned the now-seeing man once more. They challenged him to "give glory to God by telling the truth .... [They said] ... 'we know this man is a sinner'" (John 9:24). But the man said, "Whether he is a sinner or not, I don't know. One thing I do know. I was blind but now I see!" (John 9:25). Again, the man born blind simply

---

[42] There is no "J" in Hebrew. If you look in the original 1611 King Iames Bible, it is spelled Iesus. This became "Jesus" in later translations. But the Hebrew name was Yeshua, probably what He would have gone by at the time of these events.

speaks the truth. He has no reason to be deceptive to the priests and the Pharisees. But the simple truth is powerful.

For a third time, they asked him what Yeshua had done, exactly. He answered, "I have told you already and you did not listen. Why do you want to hear it again? Do you want to become His disciples too?'" (John 9:26). At this, they became angry and declared, "We are disciples of Moses! We know that God spoke to Moses, but as to this fellow, we don't even know where he comes from" (John 9:29).

Again, their anger is the result of *fear* of the new teaching that they didn't understand, and the fear of loss of position to a prophet they did not control. After all, the Pharisees knew the law and the Torah and the sayings of the prophets by rote. They followed the *letter* in a rigid, legalistic way and required the same of others. But the *spiritual truth* behind the law escaped them, just as it escaped Nicodemus when Jesus said in John 3, "You must be born again" (John 3:9–12; see also 2 Corinthians 3:14–15).

The Pharisees were bound by written words, but without spiritual sight. See 1 Corinthians 2:14–16. When Paul said, "If you are led by spirit you are not under the law" (Galatians 5:18), he did not mean the law was wrong or that reading Torah was not instructive. These things are very useful to more fully know and understand God's purpose. What he meant is that the regulations of outward conduct ("flesh"), both the law that says "thou shalt" and the law that says "thou shalt not" cannot effect the change of heart, in themselves, that is necessary for the salvation of fallen man; nor can it awaken the dormant spirit in the worldly people (see Romans 8:1–17). Someone can follow all the outward rules and ignore the inward spiritual need for *transformation*. We human beings require this *transformation* to overcome our natural weaknesses and worldliness, including spiritual blindness (see Ephesians 3:18–19; 4:7–16).

Read the Beatitudes in Matthew 5:1–10. The Pharisees were a long way from this way of being, as is practically everyone now in this twenty-first century. This is why Yeshua said, "Unless your righteousness exceeds that of the Pharisees and the teachers of the law, you will certainly not enter the kingdom of Heaven" (Matthew 5:20). You must have a changed heart and a spiritual awakening to be the person we are called to be. This was the subject of *I, Witness*, as I recounted my own spiritual awakening, and many others have had similar experiences. I do not mean it happens the same way for everyone. What is required is heartfelt belief, and that belief, in Christ, *will* change you (see Ephesians 4:11–16). Whether all at once or over a long time, it doesn't matter. He loves you, and the blood is effective. But He will *give* you a changed heart when you really believe in Him. And having the change, one will gradually become more spiritual by nature, with practice. You will see many things you missed before. And you will be overcome with joy, like Scrooge on Christmas morning.

However, following the law cannot accomplish this change, because for example, if a person lusts after women, even though he does not have sex with them, this outward obedience to the commandment not to commit adultery does *not* make him worthy of the kingdom of Heaven (Matthew 5:27–30). Here, Jesus is referring to the man who ogles every woman and makes lewd comments. And if a person were to nurse anger, hate, and bitterness in his heart, he would not be a much better person in God's eyes than one who is in prison for murder, and eventually, his bitterness might actually lead to murder or other hateful acts (Matthew 5:21–26). If someone is eaten up with envy of others' possessions, constantly wishing he had what every other one has, he is no more righteous than a thief and likely will be tempted eventually to do something dishonest. *Man in his natural state often cannot help having these failings because he lives in a fallen world.* Only a transformed, a *regenerate* person can have a state of being that allows us to even try to do Christ's teaching. Even then, it is a *process.* We try, we fail, we keep trying. *This does not negate salvation; it confirms it.*

Therefore, Paul says that salvation is by faith, not by "works of the law" (see, e.g., Romans 3:19–26; 9:32–33). A person can do the outward while having no inward connection to the spirit. A rigid legalistic practice going through the motions is not the same as knowing God, and those who do not know God cannot please Him. This is true despite ritualistic practices being carried on, however diligently. This is the message of Isaiah 1:11–22. The people made all the sacrifices, just as in Leviticus. Still, God was sick of them because they were hypocrites and did not care for the poor.

> The person without the Spirit does not accept the things that come from the Spirit of God but considers them foolishness, and cannot understand them because they are discerned only through the Spirit. (1 Corinthians 2:14)

Unfortunately, for this reason, the effort to teach the greater messages of the Bible to those who have not given themselves to Christ is often fruitless. Belief and surrender have to come first, and we suffer all the time because of pride, which we must contend with daily. But once we do surrender to Him, our eyes are opened, and we can see what we missed before (2 Corinthians 3:16).

So, Yeshua does not disrespect the Sabbath in rejecting the Pharisees' rigid legalistic interpretation. Rather, He interposes a profound respect for the *spirit* of Sabbath by ignoring the trivializing details of the Pharisees' legalistic practice and performing God's work on the Sabbath.

But wait! There's more!

The Pharisees said,

"We are disciples of Moses! But as for this other fellow, we do not know where he comes from" (John 9:29). The blind man who had received sight said, "Now that is remarkable! You don't know where he comes from, yet he opened my eyes. We know that God does not listen to sinners. He listens to the Godly person who does His will. Nobody has ever heard of opening the eyes of a man born blind. If this man were not from God, he could do nothing" (John 9:30–33). It is as though a light appeared to this man and he became the teacher, while the Pharisee teachers became the poor learners! This role reversal reflects the anointing Christ put on the healed blind man. The man born blind became the Rabbi (teacher). He also fulfilled his sending by speaking truth to power.

But more than this, we see another reason why Jesus put mud on his eyes. We have seen Yeshua heal with a word or a touch, but the mud was washed in the water of Siloam (sending). Actually, this parallels baptism *and* anointing. The saved are physically washed in baptism, and the story as it pertains to the blind man is intended to show us salvation. But the sending is emphasized by the anointing. People are often anointed when they are *sent*. And therefore, the blind man from his birth becomes the teacher. Sending is also dangerous, for we go as sheep among wolves (Mark 6:6–13).

This demonstrates how the saved (regenerate; born again) become teachers by spiritual sight. Men in stone buildings with degrees after their names may or may not have spiritual sight.[43] The Pharisees were the most educated people of that time, but they were ignorant. They had wisdom in the world, but God's foolishness is wiser than human wisdom (1 Corinthians 1:18–19). Many things in the story of the blind man also parallel the story of Yeshua's life and ministry on earth. The mud symbolizes the mud from which Adam, *who is a type for Christ* (Romans 5:14), was made. Adam was the first man made by God, not by the will of the flesh; Christ was the Second, although really, He was First (see John 1:1–4). And the washing symbolizes the baptism of Yeshua. Yeshua was sent by God (see Romans 8:3); the man born blind was sent by Yeshua, who is the Son of God. The blind man first proclaimed to his neighbors that he was given sight by Yeshua. Yeshua spent three years preaching to the people of Israel and Jerusalem that light had come into the world. The man born blind was tried by the priests and eventually found guilty, although Yeshua had already said neither he nor his parents had sinned (John 9:3). In the process, *he reversed the roles and became the priest,* offering the priests of the synagogue the opportunity to become Yeshua's disciples. ("Do you want to become His disciples too?"). At the trial and crucifixion, Christ reversed the role of Caiaphas and became the High Priest. Evidence for this is in the description of the garment over which the soldiers cast lots, a priestly garment with no seams (further, see Hebrews 7:17, where Jesus becomes the high priest). The man born blind was unfairly convicted and punished by expulsion (John 9:34). Christ then saved him, giving him what few would receive while Yeshua had not yet been crucified, elevating him from death to life (John 9:35–38 and see John 5:24). This symbolically parallels the resurrection. The man reborn with sight thus mirrors events, things

---

[43] I have met wonderful, blessed pastors with real knowledge of God and some I think with lots of bookish knowledge whose spirituality was lacking. But mostly they are sincere believers. Many, however, seem to be unable to say the things I am saying—perhaps because they are charged with keeping the pews full and the tithes coming in.

that had happened already, and things yet to come in Yeshua's life, in Baptism, anointing, sending, blamelessness, and trial and punishment in innocence, becoming the teacher of those who had been the teachers and, symbolically, the resurrection.

The blind man is also Everyman. I love the idea of Everyman. Everyman has problems, and weaknesses; he is fallen, stumbles, and is lifted by Christ. Nothing in the story indicates the blind man had learning or wisdom before his encounter with Christ. But Christ, through His power, bestowed sight. The implication is that Christ can give anyone sight, which is central to our faith that God can do what God says, as with Abraham (see Romans 4: 9–15). Though not fully revealed in the world at the time, Jesus healed the man born blind by giving him sight. The Holy Spirit was later to come into the world to teach us all things (John 14:26). Like the blind man, Everyman believes in Christ and receives life through the spirit.

Flesh and Spirit

If you are following along with your Bible or Bible app, read Romans 8:1–27. Paul tells us that:

> Therefore, there is now no condemnation for those who are in Christ Jesus, because through Christ Jesus the law of the Spirit who gives life has set you free from the law of sin and death. For what the law was powerless to do because it was weakened by the flesh[44] God did by sending His own Son in the likeness of sinful flesh to be a sin offering.[45] And so he condemned sin in the flesh in order that the righteous requirement of the law might be fully met in us who do not live according to the flesh but according to the Spirit. (Romans 8: 1–4)[46]

Paul explains that setting one's mind on the "flesh" (i.e., materialism) is hostile to God. Worldly people, meaning focused only on the material world of daily events, cannot see spiritual things; nor can they please God. We are children of God and joint heirs with Christ! (see also Galatians 3:25–29.) Because of this, we need to develop our spiritual awareness, and through the Holy Spirit, we can become spiritual people!

"The law weakened by the flesh" (Romans 8:3) means that the law could not save because of man's endless list of worldly desires and inner

---

[44] Or sinful (human) nature.
[45] In other words, human. A sin offering was one of the sacrifices commanded in Leviticus.
[46] The sin offering was one of the ritual sacrifices of the ancient Hebrews, for certain sins.

sins such as pride, envy, avarice, and lust. So that instead of bringing us to love God, the ritual sacrifices, the journeys to Jerusalem, and all that went with them became burdensome in the minds of people (see Malachi 1: 6–14). The best firstborn animal was promised, but despite outward piety, people we can imagine groaning inwardly, for hundreds of years, dozens of generations, giving for the ritual sacrifices with endless trips to Jerusalem. It was great for the priests but undoubtedly tough for the farmers. So, as Malachi 1 describes, a diseased goat was offered instead, angering God.

Also, we do not receive this spiritual sight and understanding until we have Christ, and through Him the Holy Spirit, so, we cannot "see" spiritual truth! (1 Corinthians 2:14). The blind man states, "Now that is remarkable! You don't know where he comes from, yet he opened my eyes!" (John 9:30). How can this be? The Pharisees were learned men!

God gave them a spirit of stupor, Eyes that could not see and ears that could not hear, to this very day." Romans 11:8.

Where is the wise person? Where is the teacher of the law? Where is the philosopher of this age? Has not God made foolish the wisdom of this world? (1 Corinthians 1:20)

What no eye has seen; What no ear has heard; and what no human mind has conceived—the things God has prepared for those who love Him—these are the things God has revealed to us by his Spirit. (1 Corinthians 2:9–10)

He has blinded their eyes and hardened their hearts so they can neither see with their eyes, nor understand with their hearts, nor turn—and I would heal them. (John 12:40)

Thus, shown up, the priests and scribes were proven to be ignorant because they were spiritually blind. Upon being embarrassed by the blind man, they respond with anger. They accuse the formerly blind man who has been given the gift of sight of being steeped in sin at birth and expel him from the synagogue, a harsh punishment (John 9:34). Again, this parallels Yeshua's trial and crucifixion. We already know that the blind man did not sin, nor his parents. He was sent as an instrument of God!

The Good Shepard

Jesus finds the man and asks him to believe in the Son of Man, speaking of Himself in the third person, and explains it is He, and the man worships Him! (John 9:35–38).

But then He does one more remarkable and provocative thing, in stating "For judgment I have come into this world, so that the blind will see and those who see will become blind" (John 9:39). Those who had been declaring themselves disciples of Moses, but who only could see as the world sees, heard this and said, "What? Are we blind too?" (John 9:40). Yeshua answers that if they were blind, they would be without sin, but since they claim to be able to see, their "guilt remains" (John 9:41). Compare this to the opening of the story at John 9:1-3. Who sinned? A man born blind has not sinned, but a man refusing to see and misleading the flock is the one who has sinned! Moreover, He demonstrates that salvation simply requires admitting one's blindness and humbling oneself in the presence of the Messiah.

More than this, those who "sat in the seat of Moses" were now displaced, and the Lord Jesus took the judgment seat.[47] (John 9:39). For He is the judge (see John 5:30). This was then recapitulated at the crucifixion when Caiaphas rent his garment.[48] From that point on, the earthly priesthood was void and the High Priest was Yeshua. And soon

---

[47] In other words, He is the judge of the world. Originally, before the first king, the Hebrews had judges to lead them. This establishes Jesus as the rightful leader of the Hebrews, though they do not recognize Him.

[48] According to the Hebrew tradition, the High Priest's garment must be perfect, seamless, and free from tears or patches.

after (AD 70), the worldly temple was destroyed. The new temple is Christ (Revelation 21:22).

(Ignore the fact that the next part is chapter 10; He is still talking to the same gathering. Read John 10:1-18.[49])

"Anyone who does not enter the sheep pen by the gate, but comes in some other way, is a thief and a robber" (John 10:1). Christ declares there is one plan for salvation, and only those who enter that way will be accepted (John 10:7). "I am the gate for the sheep. All who have come before me are thieves and robbers." No one else can offer what Christ offers. "Whoever enters through me will be saved" (John 10:9). The sheep follow Him because they know His voice. They do not follow a stranger because they do not know his voice (John 10:4-5). Again, it is plain as day that God's plan is Jesus Christ and only Jesus Christ. Always was and always will be (see also Ephesians 1:3-14). God's plan has been in place "from the foundations of the earth."

Jesus contrasts Himself to the hired hand. The Good Shepherd lays down his life for His sheep, but the hired hand runs away, and the wolves scatter the flock (John 10:11-15). The priesthood never recognized that they really were just hired hands, temporary help. Or rather, they rejected that their part was to guard the flock *until* the Messiah arrived; and now that He has arrived, they are no longer the ones in charge. However, they don't want to give up their positions, but they no longer have any right to hold them. Thus, the priests have lost the legitimacy of their positions because the Messiah has entered the world, and they refuse to serve Him. Yeshua made it clear when He declared, "I am the gate; Whoever enters by me will be saved" (John 10:9).

In Matthew 21:33-41, Jesus tells the Parable of the Tenants. The Master made a vineyard, surrounded it with a moat and a hedge, and put in it a wine press and a watchtower. He hired it out to tenant farmers. When the crop was ripe, he sent servants to collect the fruit, but the tenants abused and killed them, so he sent more servants, but they were treated the same way. Finally, he sent his son, saying, "They will respect my son," but the tenants conspired to kill the son and steal the

---

[49] Remember, chapter and verse numbers were not present in the original text but were added in the thirteenth and fifteenth centuries.

inheritance. The priests understood that the parable was about them at the time (Matthew 21:45).

The Hebrews were under a law specifically designed to separate them and sanctify them. This is the hedge and moat around the vineyard (or fence). This was so they would be different from the pagans; a unique people having a deep moral sense and careful traditions. The "watchtower" is the temple, set up to be a place of learning and seeing to watch for the Messiah's coming, cultivating a priest caste and men of learning like the Pharisees. The winepress represents the altar where the blood sacrifices were made. Obviously, the tenants represent the priests and teachers. The Lord sent the prophets, who were His servants, and they were killed. And when he sent more, the wicked tenants killed them too. So, He sent His Son, Jesus. The evil tenants plotted to kill Him and take the inheritance for themselves—in order to remain the rulers and leaders of the people (stealing the inheritance). The chief priests and Pharisees understood clearly that Christ was talking about them and wanted to kill Him, but they feared the people, who are the "fruit" that God wants to harvest for His kingdom (Matthew 21:45–6).

Back to John 10. The Jews (the priests and Pharisees) are divided (John 10:19–22). Some are impressed by the miracles; others think he's "demon-possessed and raving mad" (John 10:20). None fall down and worship at this time, not accepting that He is the Messiah.

> I will destroy the wisdom of the wise. (1 Corinthians 1:18, quoting Isaiah 29:14)

> But God chose the foolish things of the world to shame the wise. (1 Corinthians 1:27)

> See I lay in Zion a stone that causes people to stumble and a rock that makes them fall. (Romans 9:33)

The Pharisees knew the words carved in the *stone but were blinded to the Spirit who carved the stone.* Saying this in no way disrespects the law. The law was given to be a teacher, or protector, *until* Christ would come and we would no longer be in need because He, through the Holy

Spirit, is our teacher and protector and guide (see Galatians 4:1–7). But we are to live by the Spirit, meaning we are meant to see behind and beyond what is just written on paper or stone to even greater things the Spirit will teach us (Romans 7:1–6; See John 14:25–26; 2 Corinthians 3:4–18). Jesus was always all about the spirit. "Flesh gives birth to flesh, but Spirit gives birth to Spirit" (John 3:6). Read Romans 8:1–18: The law was weakened by the flesh (or sinful nature). How can this be? Because of the lack of spiritual sight, the distractions of the material world, and the constant demands of the flesh.

Paul was a lawyer. He knew how people who are sinners in their hearts use the law. In our twenty-first-century world, when people hire lawyers, they do it often to find ways around the law, ways to use the law for personal gain, or ways to excuse themselves for their immoral acts (See, Matthew 23:13–39). Look at Mark 7:9–13 and Malachi 1:6–14. Paul had been one of those "teachers of the law" when he witnessed with approval the stoning of Steven (Acts 7:58). Read Acts 9:1–4, Paul's persecution of the followers of Jesus, before his conversion. These things were also done in the name of the law.

In 1 Corinthians, chapters 1 and 2, Paul lays out plainly the importance of spiritual sight, as opposed to "wise words." The wisdom of the world is weak, and worldly logic and wisdom can't fix what was broken in the fall—namely, the direct intimate relationship between man and God and the ability to see and know God in the deepest spiritual sense. God said "Abraham," and Abraham said, "Here I am" (Genesis 22:1).[50] The Lord came to visit Abraham at Abraham's home with two angels (or messengers). (See Genesis 18:1–20.) When we have people who drop by casually to talk to us, we are friends and family. YHWH and Abraham were like friends.

So, what does the story tell us about getting the sight? Clearly, it is only by *knowing* Yeshua Messiah and having the Holy Spirit in us as a guide that one can receive this sight. Without this *transforming* reality, we are spiritually blind. The uneducated blind man, given sight by

---

[50] I had a friend who was a lawyer and also a church friend, who killed himself. Once I commented in adult Sunday school that I thought God speaks to everyone. He responded, "He doesn't do it in English." He was blind to the voice of God, and I was blind to his troubled spirit. God forgive us.

Yeshua, becomes the teacher to the teachers. Consider Saul's conversion also; though he was lettered and learned, he was taught his Gospel by the Holy Spirit and not by men (see Galatians 1). So the Torah was given as a teacher to men (Galatians 3:24–27), but men in their brokenness objectified the Torah. They thought following the *letter* of the law was the same thing. It isn't. Refer again to 2 Corinthians 3:4–18.

The Spirit is the law *within* the law. When the Spirit of God is in our hearts, we *fulfill* the law (see Jeremiah 31:27–34). Paul points this out in Romans 2:27–29. And also, consider the Greatest Commandment (Romans 13:8–10). We who love God and His Son and our fellowman deeply and sincerely and who live accordingly have fulfilled the law in God's sight. And in Matthew, it is written, "All the law and the prophets hang on these." And this is the law that is written on our hearts (Jeremiah 31:33–34). Rules about food and drink and special days and sacrifices do not bind the Christian (see Colossians 2:16–23, Mark 7:14–23).

Another Sabbath

I believe there is also a message here about the sabbath. In Hebrews 4:4–7, it says God completed the creation and rested "on the seventh day." But "a long time later," God spoke through David, saying, "Today if you hear His voice do not harden your hearts." Today, as opposed to the seventh day. There is another day called today:

> "There remains then a Sabbath rest for the people of God, for anyone who enters God's rest also rests from their works; just as God did from His" (Hebrews 4:9, 10).

> For, the word of God is alive and active. Sharper than any double-edged sword, it penetrates even to dividing soul and spirit, joints and marrow; it judges the thoughts and attitudes of the heart. Nothing in all creation is hidden from God's sight. Everything is uncovered and laid bare before Him to whom we must give account. (Hebrews 4:12, 13)

Therefore, we enter God's rest today as we give glory to God, as we spend time with Him, as we come to know Yeshua who saved us by His blood, as we listen for that still small voice—today! And, as it says in Hebrews 4:14, we are attended by the Great High Priest any day we call on Him with a true heart.

See also Romans 14:5–6: "One person considers one day to be more sacred than another; another considers every day alike. Each of them should be fully convinced in his own mind" (see also Colossians 2:8–17). I think they are also saying the same thing. There is a Sabbath of ritual practice and a Sabbath of the Spirit, which is greater.

I conclude from all this that, the deeper Sabbath is each of us alone with God, with the Lord Jesus, with the Holy Spirit, who is sent to teach us all things. Since we have a busy world, a day set apart (when possible) allows this to occur. It is not sent to be an empty ritual, devoid of spirit. It is not sent to be a rule to be harshly enforced, a burden carrying an additional burden of guilt, or to critique others' practices, whether it be Saturday or Sunday or any other day. Indeed, I believe it is the quiet time one takes to be with God; the day and hour are much less important than the practice. The direct individual knowledge of God found in "God's rest" is the law. Nothing can please God but that we know God, and if we know God, we will always strive to please God, and He will "remember our transgressions no more" (Jeremiah 31:34).

Yeshua died so we could have God inside us, and Yeshua is our mediator and High Priest Forever for this purpose. And the Holy Spirit is our guide and teacher. There is nothing wrong with keeping traditions, as long as tradition does not supplant the spiritual reality of God in the Sabbath today.

Last point: There is nothing wrong with people who choose to honor the Sabbath, including counting days. There are two things that are basic in all these Scriptures, though. One is honoring the Spirit of the Sabbath. It is our obligation to hear His voice through the Holy Spirit today, whether it is the seventh day of our week or the first or any other day, as long as it is today. Rigid, legalistic thinking does not get us to that scenario. That is "salvation by works." And guilt separates us from God, as we worry we are not doing Sabbath "right." This is what I think is meant by Colossians. "Therefore do not let anyone judge you by what you eat or drink, or with regard to a religious festival, a New Moon celebration or a Sabbath day" (Colossians 2:16). And we should not require others to do it "our way," either (Romans 14:4–6). Be convinced in your own mind, and do what you believe is right.

Joy

There is an old protestant hymn, "In the Garden," by C. Austin Miles, that says, "And He walks with me; And He talks with me; And He tells me I am His own; And the joy we share as we tarry there; None other has ever known." This is the blessed relationship we can each share with Christ our Savior any time just by putting aside our work for a while and opening our hearts and minds to Him.

Yes, we take up our cross and follow. We are sifted and tested. Yes, we lead clean lives, as best we can, with God's help. But we do so with joy in our hearts! God's Rest is supposed to be our wellspring of joy. And, no, we are not meant to be worldly and hold worldly "prosperity" in high regard. This joy, like living water, flows from the Holy Spirit in us, even in suffering, even in deepest sorrow. There are some preaching now a Gospel of "prosperity." Especially after my years of working with our homeless, I reject that teaching. In fact, I say between the prosperous and the homeless, I believe the homeless are much closer to God.

On a personal note, I would add that Sabbath to me brings the joy, as in the song. I take my personal Sabbath mornings, as that is my quiet time that I can spend with God. Sometimes I walk alone for an hour and pray and meditate walking. Other times, I spend it in my chair by the window with my coffee and my Bible. This is also Sabbath—to me. It is a practice, but it is not a ritual. I feel a need for it, but I do not feel guilty about it (like how I used to feel if I "skipped church" on Sunday). Some days I feel the need to continue all day; others, I am busy. It is okay! It is okay for me to be me and okay for you to be you! Take peace and joy in the fact that God loves you! This is the blessing of the Sabbath. He who wrote on the stone loved the people; our God loves us. He wants us to love Him every day. So, we can live with a glad heart, rejoicing in Him. No matter how bad things are, they are always a little better after I spend some quality time with Him.

Here is what I know for certain and have borne witness to: We are spirits, created to be perfect children of light, though we live in temporary houses of flesh. But we fall short, and we all sin because of the weaknesses of the flesh. Yeshua (Jesus Christ's name in Hebrew) came and sacrificed Himself so that I could escape the judgment for my sins. He did this out of love and grace. He laid down His life of His own accord for me. He relieved me of my burden of sin. He was my brother, but I did not know Him. Even so, He died for me. And God raised Him from the dead. He made known that if I believe in Him and look to Him and follow Him all the way to the end, I will have eternal life and escape the judgment and the second death in the lake of fire. Compared to this, what else matters?

Why Wasn't the Law of Moses the Answer?

If you read in the Bible, beginning at Mark 1:1, it starts off with John the Baptist, out in the wilderness with his disciples. John was the Herald of Christ. And everywhere, he was proclaiming the Messiah was coming. And he was preaching repentance and immersing people in water for the forgiveness of sins. People were coming from far and near to be washed and forgiven for their sins. "For I will forgive their wickedness and will remember their sins no more" (Jeremiah 31:34).

But hold on just a minute!

If people had the law of Moses, and they had made the blood sacrifices before the priests in the temple, why did they need this washing by immersion by some raggedy old man in the wilderness?

The law of Moses was given under a blessing and curse (see Leviticus 26; Galatians 3:10–14). Paraphrasing, God said, "If you will do what I say, I will be your God, and you will be my people." And he gave them all the rules when they had agreed (see Exodus 19:3–7). But no one was able to bear it (Acts 15:10–11, Galatians 3:10–11)—and they did many wrong things (see Isaiah 1:1–22, Malachi 1:5–14, Mark 7:6–13). Rather, through the law, people of conscience became aware of sin (Romans 3:20). Further, the sacrifices were for sins committed inadvertently or by mistake (Leviticus 4:2), and later found out and repented (see Hebrews 7:22, 8:6, 9:23–24). Serious sins of the intentional kind, which are harmful to someone, can result in more severe penalties (Hebrews 9:11–14). (see Exodus 21 for examples).

The Torah had another purpose as well. Reading closely Matthew 21:33–46, the Parable of the Tenants, you see the vineyard is Israel; the hedge and moat (or fence) are the Torah; designed to set the people apart[51] the winepress is the altar; and the watchtower is the temple, where one could watch for those whom God would send. The priesthood were the hired hands. The reason I go into this explanation again is that some people are confused about the meaning of this parable, but Scripture states the priests understood very well that it referred to them and they were planning to kill Yeshua (see Matthew 21:33–46).

But why would God go to all this trouble if the Torah were not the final answer? Yeshua, as stated previously, was always the plan. There was not, is not and never will be a plan B. God's plans are perfect, but He was not inclined to set His Son just anywhere or among just any tribe of people. He wanted a proper place and people for His Messiah, His Son. Furthermore, YHWH, in giving this law, gave a guardian and a curator to the people[52]—who were to be the first beneficiaries when His Son would enter the world in the flesh—and to prepare them to be a nation of priests and a holy people.[53]

In the day of Moses, there was no Israel; there were no Jews. There was a multitude who came out of Egypt, a motley crew of whom half were physical descendants of Abraham. God brought them directly to Sinai and gave them their law; their religion, identity, cultural norms, rituals, and rules for living, even hygiene and interpersonal dimensions; and political system—all in one piece, as no people ever had before. To what purpose?

The logical explanation is that He was creating the place where He intended to send His Son so He could gather unto Himself all He had created. This is the harvest in the parable. Now, though, what about those outside the hedge? The answer to that question is perfectly clear because he promised Abraham that his "seed" would bless all the nations

---

[51] Rules like forbidding eating with uncircumcised, dietary restrictions, forbidding intermarrying, etc.

[52] Galatians 3:23-29.

[53] There is a lot more to the law than this. I am making this simple intentionally so that everyone can understand it. I do not want to get hung up on dogma or debates about the "debatable matters."

(plural, i.e., first the Jews and then the gentiles; see Genesis 22:16–18, Galatians 3:6–9, John 10:16, Acts 10–11, Matthew 22, Acts 13 and 15). There are many more references to this. These are just examples.

For the blood of animals cannot work the forgiveness of sin or transformation of our animal nature (see Hebrews 10:1–4). But Yeshua's blood is perfect and was freely given. Thus, God gave to him the power to lay down His life and take it up again (John 10:18). And by this, God outsmarted the devil, for having died once, death has no more dominion over him (see Romans 6:9).

But what of the institutions of churches and stone buildings we make for Christ? At the transfiguration, Peter said (paraphrasing), "This is great. Let's build three temples. One for Moses, one for Elijah, and one for you!"[54] (Matthew 17:1–8). God had a different plan. For Christ's Temple is in the heart of the believer, and our temple is in the Spirit of the Lord. I credit one of my homeless friends with pointing this out. Moses had three temples: the tent of Moses, the Temple of Solomon, and the Second Temple—and now he has many, but the light therein is diminished because of the greater light that has been revealed (see 2 Corinthians 3:4–11).

In saying these things, I am not implying my friends in institutional churches are not saved. Not at all. I am saying that it is not the worldly building that saved them or the worldly minister or the earthly priests; it is *grace* through *faith* in Christ and only that which saved them. And that is not property of a human institution to dispense but is the gift of Jesus Christ, dispensed to the believer directly, whether he goes to worship in a fancy stone building or on his knees in a foxhole, or in prison, or in the cancer ward. I saw one of our homeless men kneeling beside his bed, praying earnestly for an exceptionally long time the other night. Jesus is very much present in the homeless shelter.

Paul makes clear in all his letters that while the law of Moses was, in fact, good, for only good things come from God, it has served the purpose for which God gave it to Israel. That is to be Israel's teacher, guardian, and disciplinarian to prepare the world for the entry of Christ.

---

[54] There is a tendency for those whose eyes have been newly opened to become overly exuberant, say silly things, or be insensitive to the fact that not everyone is going to be on the same page. I was also guilty of this, just like Peter in this story.

This was always God's plan. There was never any "plan B." God's plans are perfect. Now that we have Christ, eternal life, and the Holy Spirit, we no longer need a guardian or disciplinarian (Galatians 4:1–7). And the purpose of the law has been *fulfilled*.

He created a place for us. "In the beginning, God created the heavens and the earth" (Genesis 1:1). And he put us here in these bodies of flesh. And likewise, He created a place for Jesus Christ to appear and to bring us home to Him at the time of the harvest. It is simple. It was always simple. We were planted, and we will be reaped. That which confuses it is the devil.

> But in fact the ministry Jesus has received is as superior to theirs as the covenant of which he is mediator is superior to the old one, since the new covenant is established on better promises. (Hebrews 8:6)

And this is the reason we must be able to enter God's presence, not only on a certain day or predetermined time but *today*. If we hear his voice and do not harden our hearts, we can respond, and salvation is waiting. I simply cried, "Jesus, help me!"

And He appeared to me in a vision and said, "I thought you'd never ask." He had been waiting patiently all my life for me to make that choice! (You might find He is waiting for you as well.) To give it all up to Him, to surrender completely, knowing you just can't go another step without him—this is another answer to the purpose of suffering, disease, war, famine, and disaster, for then we see more clearly and can lose our pride and false pretenses.

I am blessed to know that we can be physically any place, any time, and perceive the calling of the Lord and receive the blessing. Because of Jesus Christ and the blood that was shed, we can have a pipeline directly to God if we approach in all seriousness, repentance, and humility and if we surrender our old life to be buried with him; then, we are raised in our *baptism* a new creation (see Romans 6:1–10, Ephesians 2:1–10). Then we can be filled with the Holy Spirit. Over time, if we persevere walking in the Spirit, we will no longer be slaves to fear, anxiety, and depression. By stages, we become more and more spiritual and less and less worldly.

It's a process, and it is ongoing. It is called "sanctification." We must be refined and tested by fire, like silver in a crucible. Faith has to be tested to be certain. We are thrashed and sifted. Our kernel is saved, and our chaff goes in the fire. What is good becomes better, and what is useless is thrown out.

Thus, having believed—the essential first step (see John 5:24)—we grow stronger in Christ in spirit, day by day. I can tell you only my experience. It is a growing and wonderful feeling. I just have to watch my pride, and refuse to let Satan confuse me with fear when the hard testing comes. I was recently tested with a very painful illness and things that went with that. God did get me through, and He never left me.

Pride has been the downfall of many good people. So, I try not to make anything special of myself, knowing it would be a lie. Nothing good has happened to me because I was good, but many things have happened because God is good. The only commendation I make for myself is that I try to do what He wants as well as I can, as well as I understand it. And if I am ever wrong, I apologize. I don't think I'm wrong about any of the important stuff. And as I accept my inevitable physical death and loss of everything in this temporary form of existence, fear gradually loses its grip.

The Gospel as Paul Taught It

I do not claim to know anything myself, but I base everything I say (that is not from direct life experience) on the Bible. However, Paul was taught not by men but by the Holy Spirit (see Galatians 1). He met the Risen Christ on the road to Damascus and was given the sight and the Spirit (Acts 9, Galatians 1). From then on, he lived entirely to teach the Gospel wherever he was sent. He was like the man born blind. He was beaten, whipped, scourged, stoned, and left for dead, shipwrecked, imprisoned, and ultimately, beheaded for it. Still, he considered these sufferings minor and temporary—considering the salvation he had been given.

Before his miraculous conversion, Paul was a Pharisee. He had to have memorized the Torah and all the scriptures of Hebrew law and tradition for that, and he excelled, for he stated he was advanced in Judaism beyond other men his age. And he burned with passion for the Jewish law and way of life, pursuing and persecuting people of the Way for what he previously saw as blasphemy.[55] But God used him as His instrument. He and people he recruited into the faith were primarily responsible for spreading Christianity into the wider world, to Greece and what is now Turkey and all around the Eastern Mediterranean and finally to Rome itself. In addition, he wrote a major portion of the New Testament, books that were originally letters to the churches and have now been incorporated into the Bible as we know it. In them, he sets out the logic and rationale for the birth, death, and resurrection of the Messiah, Jesus Christ. He sets forth how Christians should live,

---

[55] What the original Christians called themselves.

worship, and relate to one another and to other people. Indeed, it is hard to imagine Christianity without his contribution. But God *chose* him from the beginning, and He who knows all and sees all never fails and His plans are always complete in every detail.

In 1 Corinthians, Paul states he came preaching a simple Gospel, and not with wise words, lest the cross be emptied of its power.

> Jews demand signs, and Greeks look for wisdom, but we preach Christ crucified: a stumbling block to Jews and foolishness to Gentiles, but to those whom God has called, both Jews and Geeks, Christ the power of God and the wisdom of God. For the foolishness of God is wiser than man's wisdom, and the weakness of God is stronger than human strength. (1 Corinthians 1:22–25)

Acts 13 sets forth the Gospel Paul preached verbatim. Not only in Pisidian Antioch but every place he visited. On the Sabbath, he went to the synagogue and listened to the words of Moses and the prophets. Then he would rise and tell the story of Jesus and proclaim the arrival of the long-awaited Messiah. He would tell how the leaders in Jerusalem had crucified Him but that God had raised Him from the dead. And that He had come to bring eternal life to all who believed. Some of the Jews accepted him, but many did not, so he would next go to the gentiles (some of whom believed in YHWH but did not practice as the Jews, while others followed the pagan gods), and many of them who heard the good news believed in Jesus and were saved. Paul would often stay for a long time with these believers and start a church or assembly, meeting in homes and worshiping God.

In Romans 3 and 4, Paul gives a summary of redemptive history. He describes the human condition, as men were aware of God's presence from the beginning but did not worship Him. Thus, they were slaves to sin and death. And the Jews had the law, but they could not live up to the law, and so, they were no better off than the heathens. For all people fell short of God's glory. But through the law, we were made aware of sin (Romans 3:19–20). But now, God has given us another way of attaining righteousness, through faith in Jesus Christ (Romans 3:21–26).

Paul explains how it was that Abraham believed God, that Sarah would conceive and bear a child even though they were a hundred years old. And he believed it was counted to him as righteousness. This was before he was circumcised, so that through him both those who are physical descendants and those who are not but are his heirs in spirit would all benefit from the promise (Romans 4:1–12). Paul means that physical circumcision is irrelevant, a changed heart and belief in Jesus are the things that matter. And the promise is the blessing of salvation and forgiveness of sins—a fresh start and a clean slate.

And he explains that the promises to Abraham are *inherited* by the Christian believers through faith in Christ (Romans 3:13–25, Galatians 3:15–20, Galatians 4:6–7). And Paul spent the rest of his life preaching the good news.

Above all, Paul preached a Gospel of love (1 Corinthians 13:13). "And now these three remain: faith, hope and love. But the greatest of these is love" (see also Romans 12:11–21, Romans 13:8–10). God loves us and wants us to love one another just as we love our children and want them to love one another.

So, this was *always* God's plan. From the creation to the present and the future. One plan, one salvation (Ephesians 1:1–14). The law was given as part of preparing the people and the place He would send Yeshua, the Messiah. Once Yeshua came and performed His work here and ascended into Heaven, the law had *fulfilled* its purpose (see Ephesians 2:11–22). For the true believers are led by the Spirit.[56] And this is why we have to become more spiritual people.

Hopefully at this point, you see God's plan and the miraculous gifts that are included for us. God created man; sin entered the world; and God created a place and a people to send His Son, Jesus. Jesus brought life, spiritual awakening, and resurrection for His people. In His death and resurrection, He broke the power of Satan, and his reign of sin and death. Christ gives us sight; He sent us a "superpower" called the Holy Spirit, which we call upon for aid in all situations. He changes our hearts and minds.

---

[56] See appendix for summary.

In the last part, I hope to answer the questions of why we still need to suffer, how we are expected to live, and what it is like trying to be the person Christ intended us to be while still being weak, fallible, and prone to sin.

PART THREE

Walking the Walk—Essays on Christian Living

Why the Homeless?[57]

Why are the homeless so important to me? Yes, they are human beings, and a good person should give alms. But I am not talking in those terms; that is how the world sees them. One homeless person said, "You know why I respect you, Joe? It is because most people look at me, and they see a homeless person. You look at me, and you just see a person."

He is kind of a philosopher of the street. And he has it almost right about me. I look at him, and I see a mirror. A little sleight-of-hand here, a small twist of fate there, and he would easily have been the respectable attorney, while I could easily have become an educated street person. As I said in *I, Witness*, I was already on that path at one point, and had I not changed direction, I might have become a forty–year-old alcoholic on the street, under the bridge, in a shelter. In fact, one of the books I carried around with me in my vagabond pilgrimage states exactly that. I thought it was the way to spiritual and emotional resurrection after all the pain I had endured and lack of lasting love in this life, the cruelty of the world, the awfulness with which people are treated. But something about those guys in that alley behind a liquor store in Erie, Pennsylvania, struck a note and convinced me that I did not want to be them in ten years or less.[58] And God's hand gave me a nudge on another path. But that is the superficial part.

---

[57] Other people will have different callings. I realize my calling is not for everyone, and each of us has different gifts. But these people are the ones whom God called me to serve, and this is an example of what happens when we are led by the Spirit and It puts us to work in the world.
[58] This is one of the life learning experiences I described in *I, Witness*, the story of my personal encounter with Jesus Christ and how it changed my life.

Going deeper (this is a deep faith journey), our society, twenty-first-century America, has become a society that resembles Israel in the late First Temple period. Some have compared us to Rome, but it is worse than that. For, "From everyone who has been given much, much will be demanded" (Luke 12:48).

The Hebrews of Judah and Israel, of old Jerusalem, had been entrusted with the oracles of God (Romans 3:2). These were the people Moses had gone up on the mountain for and received the tablets of stone. In fact, God had taken them by the hand and led them out of Egypt (Jeremiah 11:1–7). He had been a husband to them, and they had been unfaithful, worshipping pagan idols even in the temple. Further, they had become prideful—the women walked around with outstretched necks (Isaiah 3:16). Men offered unclean sacrifices (Malachi 1:6–12).

But the worst sin of all was the way they treated one another. They neglected the widow, the orphan, the poor, the elderly (Isaiah 1:21–23). They were grinding the faces of the poor (Isaiah 3:15). This is when we look down on people, treat them as "other" or "less than." Be careful. God loves them. They are not "less than."

And God allowed Nebuchadnezzar to destroy the city and the temple and slaughter and enslave them. Their king was led out by hooks in his nose. The Temple of Solomon was razed to the ground. Most of their young men and many others had died by the sword. The land was raped, plundered. Field and streets were drenched in blood. Worst of all, God spirited away the ark, the tablets, the jar of mana, the rod of Aaron—the original group of sacred elements from the temple-and brought them to heaven (Revelation 11:19).

By analogy, when the Pilgrims were brought here, they were followers of the *same* God, the mighty one of Israel. They were no more numerous than the family of Abraham, which went into Egypt 430 years before Moses. In fact, only half of them survived the passage and the first winter. North America was sparsely populated. The Pilgrims and many others who came here came specifically to escape religious persecution and to pursue the word of God and the way of Christ according to their consciences. And they were given land, progeny, and a blessing just like the promises to Abraham long ago (Genesis 22:16–18). There were both a physical hedge of protection in the oceans that were long, difficult crossings in wooden ships; and I personally believe also a spiritual one, for the believers who risked everything to come here for Him were like Abraham, in simple obedience coming out of the land of Ur so long ago. How far we have fallen!

> See how the faithful city has become a prostitute! She once was full of justice; righteousness used to dwell in her—but now murderers! Your silver has become dross; your choice wine is mixed with water. Your rulers are rebels, partners of thieves; They all love bribes and chase after gifts. They do not defend the cause of the fatherless; the widow's case does not come before them. (Isaiah 1:21–23)

Jesus wept! As I said in *I, Witness, our country has become a society that throws away human beings.* We throw away more things than any people who ever lived. People in Venezuela and some places in Africa would be able to live by eating what we put in the garbage and set out for the refuse collectors. Some of the homeless can tell you where the best dumpsters are, where they can usually be fed from what is thrown out. And paper! I get a basket of paper and cardboard in the mail almost daily. Much of it is unwanted solicitations, unnecessary pieces of paper, envelopes I never even open. But worse by far is that we treat human beings the same way. I use "we" meaning our society as a whole.

I do not want to go into politics, but consider abortion. In some places, full-term babies can *legally* be killed, either terminated right before birth or left to die immediately after. Other places, this happens at various stages of gestation. This is a total sinful disregard of God's creation. Please do not think I lack empathy and understanding with women, especially those who are abused and left to raise a child they never wanted. I do recognize that the offspring of these situations may also suffer in life. However, this does not justify killing any more than the former practices of killing the young during a famine or killing the disabled. It is the reverence for God's ultimate creation and a tenderness of heart toward the helpless and disadvantaged that I believe is a cornerstone of Christianity—and of our humanity—which is incompatible with killing an innocent baby.

In fact, America has become a nation of murderers through a trick of the devil. A group of lawyers called the Supreme Court misapplied laws intended to enhance the sanctity of *individual* human lives and to respect the integrity and dignity of the *individual*. The values reflected in the Declaration of Independence and Constitution make no mention of the "greater good." These laws were written to promote individual human rights.[59] They have been twisted to do exactly the opposite. So now, the tenderest and weakest people can be treated exactly the way we treat used paper products. And this persists in our land—sometimes even government funded.

Also, Americans, as a nation, have become sex addicts. Removing from the reproductive act the "punishment" (as stated by President Obama) of children, we are free to engage in endless physical stimulation, flooding our little brains with oxytocin (one of our feel-good brain chemicals that triggers orgasm) as often as we please with no regard for any potential unwanted responsibilities. We have become a nation of perpetual teenagers, obsessed with physical beauty, finery, possessions, and regarding unlimited sex as some kind of accomplishment. "So, God gave them over to their degrading passions" (Romans 1:26).

But, of course, we also have "slip-ups" (in other words, unwanted children). And what do we do with them? Some are just abused and neglected, and in many cases, they are taken by the state and put in foster care. But in so many cases, the foster care leaves them broken when they "age out." Not to discount the success stories and adoptions as family members—those are wonderful—but many are also in jails, prisons, and homeless shelters, still broken, still addicted, many the children of addicted parents, never having achieved adult socialization.

Society just disowns these people. Sociologists and psychologists have all kinds of explanations for this, but a lack of Christianity is

---

[59] I understand that the part of the Constitution that compromised with the slave states was wrong and incompatible with the good things that were in those documents. We live in a fallen world, and the devil always tries to lay traps, especially when we attempt to do good. And the treatment of black people has also been an abomination at times. It is hard to erase these stains. The entire country has suffered and continues to suffer because of this.

paramount in my thinking. Jesus Christ was especially drawn to the poor. He said, "Whatever you do to these the least of my brothers, you also do to me" (Matthew 25:34–46). Hello! If you do not care about these people—the poor, the old, the prisoner, the homeless, the orphan—then you do not know Jesus!

When you fall on your knees, when you give your heart to Jesus 100 percent, when you say "my life for you," then your eyes are opened. When you are filled with the Holy Spirit, then you see the truth.[60] "God is spirit and must be worshiped in spirit and in truth" (John 4:24).

"Wash and make yourselves clean. Take your evil deeds out of my sight; stop doing wrong. Learn to do right; seek justice. Defend the oppressed. Take up the cause for the fatherless; plead the case for the widow" (Isaiah 1:16–17).

But what do we good people do? Instead of following God's directive, we lodge complaints against the homeless. We send the police to break up their camps, seize their tents and belongings. We complain to the city and to the county about having shelters in "our" neighborhoods. We refuse to rent to people with low credit scores or police records. We buy up affordable housing and turn it into expensive condominiums and places the poor cannot afford to rent. And thus, homelessness rises. And this is how we oppress the homeless. This is how we "grind the faces of the poor" (Isaiah 3:15). Further, society treats them as "other," less than—the unwashed, the untouchable, the unwanted, the unloved, and the discarded. "But God chose the lowly things of this world and the despised things—and the things that are not—to nullify the things that are, so that no one may boast before him" (1 Corinthians 1:27–28).

So, our Lord, Jesus Christ, and people whose eyes have been opened, like the man born blind, see the homeless for who they are. They are me and you, and they are like brothers to Jesus Christ! For "the Son of Man has no place to lay his head" (Matthew 8:20).

Some people also think that the programs of state and federal

---

[60] This is how it worked for me anyway. Your experience might be unique, but something along these lines, happens for the saved people. It might happen all at once or over time; it might involve a powerful once-in-a-lifetime experience, more than one experience, or a growing awareness. I don't discount how anyone got here. I just pray for everyone to know Him.

government should be sufficient along with taxes we pay to "deal with poverty and homeless problems." It is ironic that Scrooge in Dickens' *A Christmas Carol* made the same argument.

Three years ago, when I did the "Walmart" (i.e., handing out donated clothing) job at the shelter, there were a few who enjoyed making me run back and forth when they did not really want anything. I still did it cheerfully and happily. A young man asked me about that the other day. The truth is I never minded because no matter what I did there, I still served the Lord. So, the prideful response that would have objected or refused did not come into it. Christ could have objected to the rod, to the scourge, or to the thorns—but He bore them in silence as he was poor in spirit, empowered by His grace. I pray before I go to work for the Holy Spirit to be in me and to fill me up, and I think God does send that Spirit to help us doing His work. I can't achieve that on my own through my own effort or practice, but He can lend me a drop of His grace for His task. And as I said, I think the homeless are special to Jesus.

Belief and Faith—
Related but Different

I hope by this point that you, the reader, are feeling encouraged and that your spiritual sight—if it were taking a nap—is wide awake. Amen.

Faith is not the same thing as belief. The Bible clearly states that one who believes in his heart in Jesus and looks to Him will be saved (John 6:40, Romans 10:9). But that is not all there is. Through the Holy Spirit, we can have superpowers. We can do things we never dreamed, go where angels fear to tread, with *faith*. "Clinging" to belief is like going up in an airplane. If nothing goes wrong, you believe you will come safely to a landing, and this is what you pray for. "God, keep this airplane safe." Amen. Now picture the pilot telling you the plane is going to crash and handing you a parachute. You have never done this before. You are not sure you can. "What if I don't do it right? What if the chute doesn't open? Where will I land?"

This is analogous to a "clinging" belief. White-knuckled, clutching the King James Bible, afraid that any other translation might disturb the delicate balance, springing at anyone on FB who offers an unfamiliar opinion. Or the churchgoing, rule-following kind of belief that says, "I have to go to this building, every Sunday, pay this tithe, do all the things they tell me, and I will go to heaven when I die." This sort of belief is a slippery critter. The tighter you hold on, the harder it gets. It can desert you entirely, which was essentially my experience. Understanding helps. Both getting deep into the word and having a circle of Christian friends who share experiences and insights and support is very useful. Singing and praying in groups also helps keep you open to the Spirit.

Faith takes time to grow. It starts with belief that leads to *surrender of my entire existence to Him* and ultimately leads to a life of faith led by the Holy Spirit. As Paul points out, you died to sin, so how is it possible to go on sinning? (Romans 6:1–4). But more than this, God will call you just as He called Abraham, and where He calls, we must go. What will you do there? What the Bible says: help the poor, feed the hungry, care for the sick, and tell people about Him and what He did for us, and the rewards will come to you and will be more than compensation for whatever you give—even life itself.

I skipped over Hebrews 11 earlier, and I want to recommend it to you now. It was by faith that Noah built his ark (Hebrews 11:7). It was by faith Abraham was called from the land of his birth (Hebrews 11:8). It was by faith that Moses crossed the Red Sea (Hebrews 11:29). It was by faith that David slew Goliath (Hebrews 11:32–33). And many other things happened, listed in Hebrews 11.

That faith still exists. It was by faith that the Pilgrims crossed the Atlantic Ocean to have freedom to worship Jehovah in a new world. It was by Faith that Corrie Ten Boom shared the Gospel with her fellow prisoners right under the Nazis' noses. It was by faith that the Polish people overthrew Communist rule without firing a shot. It was by faith that Martin Luther King led black people across that bridge in Selma, Alabama.

Now picture yourself, still in the plane, clinging white-knuckled in the doorway, praying to be filled with the courage of the Holy Spirit. And then imagine being filled with the Holy Spirit, letting go, leaving the safe place, drifting out into space, counting down, pulling the cord, and feeling the chute open. Rolling with the landing like a pro. The Holy Spirit can do that if you have faith. It's not easy; it's an ultimate test, and sometimes it is more like having cancer, putting our worldly existence in a doctor's hands and putting our spirit in Jesus' hands. *Notice though that you have to have faith, but it is the Holy Spirit who does it.* Not you alone, not me alone. Faith is essential, and through faith, we can call on the Holy Spirit when we need help living Godly lives and doing His work. (No, I do not advocate putting God to the test with daredevil activities like skydiving just to demonstrate our faith. The Holy Spirit does not belong to us. It is a *gift*, not to be misused.) But, by analogy, our physical bodies are like the airplane: they are going to crash sooner than you expect. Jesus Christ is the only parachute I know of.

In my life, it was things like going into the homeless shelter, making friends with people that a lot of people cross the street to avoid; giving everything I could in every way to be part of something for them in honor of God's call, pandemic notwithstanding. It begins with listening and believing God will call you—and when He does, obeying His word. Not a token, not just a check. Up and going for it, knowing "you" cannot but with *faith*, He can! Faith walks into dangerous territory, does things outside of the comfort zone, always listening for the word of God for direction. Listen for God's call. Obey Him. Ask the Holy Spirit to give you the tools you need, strength, courage, and believing He will.[61] Amen.

---

[61] Again, I stress, everyone has different gifts. What is right for me may not be God's use for you. Wait for Him, listen to Him. The Spirit will guide you to something and empower you to do what God intends.

Grace and Humility

Grace is paramount. Grace and humility are twin sisters. Grace lets other people go first. Grace forgives. Grace is kind and compassionate. Christ forgave His executioners. He saved a thief as He was dying on the cross. He prayed for us who came later. He washed the disciple's feet. Grace.

To be humble is to be small. Paulus means humble or small. Therefore, Paul (whose given name was Saul) chose that name. Because to be big carries with it the risk of pride and pride kills. Therefore, the Holy Spirit made me go to the shelter anonymously.[62] To go as a lawyer would have been to put myself on a stepstool above those I want to serve. How can you be a servant if you stand above those you serve? A servant is lowly. A servant is humble. Christ won the world by putting himself below us though He was above us—and by putting Himself behind us, though he was ahead of us. He who would lead must follow (see Matthew 20:24–28).

The truth is I need my friends more than they need me. And the blessings I receive from my work are ten times and hundred times whatever I give. The Holy Spirit has filled my heart to overflowing, and I have learned from them a great deal about living and dying. Things I just cannot express because they have to be experienced.

Grace is God's offering of salvation to sinners, Christ accepting voluntarily his death on the cross (John 10:18, Hebrews 2:14). In our

---

[62] It was two years later I revealed myself, because they needed other kinds of assistance, I was able to give, so I had to do that. I still as much as I can keep it under wraps, and do the service I was called to as humbly as I can. Most of the guests and staff still don't know anything about me. It is liberating for me as well.

daily life, it can be as simple as holding the door for someone or letting another car get in front of you in traffic. But in a greater sense, Grace forgives, grace sacrifices, not just for family and friends—many people do that—but for humanity. For strangers and for God.

"Offer your bodies a living sacrifice, holy and pleasing to God" (Romans 12:1). In Romans 12, Paul describes Christian life in straight, easy-to-understand language.

"Bless those who persecute you" (Romans 12:14).

"Do not repay anyone evil for evil" (Romans 12:17).

"Do not take revenge ... but leave room for God's wrath" (Romans 12:19).

"Do not be overcome by evil, but overcome evil with good" (Romans 12:21).

These words are not hard to understand. Sometimes it is hard to do. They describe a life that is completely different from that of most modern people. Contemporary American culture does not always let other people go first. Sometimes we are selfish to the point of greed. Sometimes we are prideful. Sometimes we are vain. Sometimes we seek vengeance and not forgiveness.

And giving alms cannot atone. The truth is that we cannot atone for our sins; that is what the "works of the law" tried to do through animal sacrifices (see Romans 3:20, Galatians 3:11). It is like "the blood of bulls and rams" (Hebrews 7:11–17, Hebrews 10:1–18, Isaiah 1:11–18). Paul explained in Hebrews (which we covered in that chapter) the reasons why this was not effective to clean our slate before God or to clear our consciences from our past sins. *Only* the blood of Christ shed on the cross can do that. It is what He died to do. No ritual in church or the tabernacle of Moses can erase the guilt of our sinful mistakes in life or free the human conscience; these are no more effective than the offering of diseased animals at the temple of God (Malachi 1:6–12). Christ is the gate, the door, the only way (John 10:7, 14:6).

So, charitable "works" do not by themselves atone for our sinful nature. No! Only in the blood of The Lamb of God can there be a pure, unblemished, and holy sacrifice (Hebrews 9:1–18). And it sanctifies and makes holy those who accept it (Hebrews 10:19–25). Jesus said, "Unless you eat the flesh of the son of man and drink his blood you have no life in you. Whoever eats my flesh and drinks my blood has eternal life and I will raise them up at the last day" (John 6:53–54). But it is not just the eating of a wafer in a church building that He is talking about. It is living a Christian life—being kind, helping others, dropping worldly self-centeredness, and becoming spiritual and selfless by degrees through work and prayer and love.

He who takes Jesus Christ and surrenders his life to Him puts to death the body of sin, and raises up a new creation in Christ, forgiven for everything he has done in the past; the old person no longer lives but the new lives in Christ (2 Corinthians 5:16–17). But it is not just "one and done"; we must serve Him and do His teaching to the end (see, for example, Revelation 2:26).

It was God who breathed into the nostrils of Adam and put the spirit of life into him (Genesis 2:7), and it is Christ who breathes into the saved the Holy Spirit and gives them a *transformed life*. Thus, rebirth is not a matter of flesh or of being born out of the womb of a mother, but it is indwelling of a new spirit that transforms and sanctifies a person (John 3:3–10, Romans 6:1–6).

Even writing this, I realize how prideful I still am. Sadly, I realize that even when I mean to do good, I still sin. As Paul describes in Romans 7:7–25, I struggle with sin. I do thank God for including this description of our plight in Scripture; it is a comfort to me.

And Peter, (I call him "the apostle of Everyman"[63]) frequently erred. He erred at the Transfiguration in wanting to build worldly temples. He wavered, trying to walk on the water. He denied Christ three times. He erred in shunning the uncircumcised in Galatians chapter 2. Yet, it was he who was the rock of the church, who performed the miracles of Christ, who spoke first at the Pentecost, who first baptized Gentiles (see Acts 10). And he was also crucified for it.

---

[63] I nicknamed him this because he makes mistakes, like Everyman.

By their examples, and by the words of Christ in Revelation 2 and 3 to the seven churches; we know that the process of preparation for the kingdom *begins* with being saved and baptized. What follows is to be purified in the fire as gold and silver; to be threshed, sifted, and relieved of our dross and chaff; and to be pruned as branches of the true vine (see John 15:1–7). No one is perfected instantly; it is prideful to think of oneself more highly than we ought (Romans 12:3).

Yes, it is a great comfort to know that I am saved and my sins forgiven. But I am by no means a finished product. If I stay true and run my race to the end; if I persevere and do not quit, then and only then will the God who created the universe call me to himself as acceptable (Revelation 3:11–13). But if I am lukewarm, Christ will spit me out of his mouth! (Revelation 3:16). For many seeds fall on shallow soil and sprout but do not grow (Mark 4:1–20). Growth is painful.

> Not only so, but we also glory in our sufferings, for we know that suffering produces perseverance; perseverance, character; and character, hope. (Romans 5:3.)

> Therefore, we do not lose heart. Though outwardly we are wasting away, yet inwardly we are being renewed day by day. (2 Corinthians 4:16–17)

> For, we know that if the earthly tent we live in is destroyed, we have a building from God, an eternal house in heaven, not built by human hands. (2 Corinthians 5:1)

> For we live by faith, not by sight. (2 Corinthians 5:7)

So, we are therefore embarked on a journey that leads us deeper and deeper into faith and away from worldliness. And as we grow and develop in Christian life as saved people, we are less of this worldly existence every day and more of the spiritual existence that endures past the body. And we know that if we die in our "tent" of flesh, Christ will raise us up at the last day with a new body (John 6:40). I should state openly that when I speak about Christians, I am referring to the saved. If you are not saved, you are not yet a Christian; you are a seeker of Christ. Better to be a seeker of Christ than a seeker after the world, because if you persist, you will find Him. You just have to believe.

Saved and Sanctified—
Related but Not the Same

I am perhaps being overly bold in saying what someone must do to be saved. My experience came as a gift from God, like every other worthwhile thing I have, and none of it was earned. None was deserved. It was simply received, as a newborn receives mother's milk (see Romans 4:1–8). However, I am afraid that everyone is not taught this way. Further, I fear not every church teaches it simply and straightforwardly to their young people. And the vast multitudes who do not even go to church have at most a vague idea how it works. So, that is why I put it in. Saved people already know these things, and they are plainly and clearly set forth in the Bible. So, feel free if you know you are saved to skip it.

First, and above all else, you must *believe* Christ is the son of God and that God raised him from the dead (John 5:24, Romans 10:9, John 6:29). Second, you must have a *repentant* heart knowing your own sin and wanting to throw off the garment of worldliness and clothe yourself with the garment of Christ (see Matthew 22:11–14).[64] You must decide to live for Christ, knowing all else is fruitless.[65] You will likely lose friends, and there will be other costs as well. You must *surrender* your

---

[64] Has your life gotten a little out of control? Are you drinking or using drugs? Maybe you are unhappy or never seem to get where you want to go or feel that life hasn't been fair to you? Maybe a changed view of the world and a new purpose is what you need. If you have read this far, you may have seen some things you do that could be part of the cause of your unhappiness. You can change your circumstances, and still not be happy—or you can let God really change you and find joy and peace serving Him.

[65] See Ecclesiastes 2:1–11.

life to Christ, your Lord. In practice, all these usually occur pretty much simultaneously, as anyone knowing who Christ is and believing in Him is going to naturally follow Him, turn from their old life of sin and join Him, transformed by the Holy Spirit. But for some, it may be more of a process. I am not excluding anyone—believe in Jesus the Son of God and believe God raised Him from the dead, and you will be saved (Romans 10:9). If anyone does those things, they should ideally be baptized as soon as possible and proclaim them to the world. He who takes Christ into himself also abides in Christ and Christ abides in him (Romans 6:1-4, John 6:44-52).

But one cannot willfully go on sinning, especially in one's heart, or take the cup of salvation cynically, without truly intending to change. This is the difference. You cannot serve Christ and just go on sinning as if nothing happened and expect to be saved (Romans 6:1-23). But neither can you be perfect despite your best efforts (Romans 7:4-24). This, in practice, is hard stuff. You could say, "Lord, I believe," but if you are not repentant in your heart and willing to take up your cross and follow, it will not stick. This requires daily practice and effort.

There is a wide gulf between inadvertent sin which we cannot help, and sin which we willfully commit, knowing that it is wrong and having the choice. I was recently tempted to gain a benefit for myself and for my wife, by obtaining the vaccine for the Covid 19, but it would have required a "little white lie." At first, I was ecstatic, but then, alarm bells went off in my head, because I know every lie, no matter our intentions, is wrong.

No, I am not perfect. Far from. For, I still become angry when I should not. I still say things I should not say. I still become prideful. All these things are sin, but try as I might, sometimes I stumble into sin without meaning to—without knowing, without plan or intent. As Paul points out in Romans 7, if I sin without intending to sin, it is not me, but sin dwelling within me that does it.[66] However, if I know that something is wrong and I intentionally do it anyway, that is breaking faith with Christ.

---

[66] Check out Genesis 4; sin crouching at the door waiting to pounce!

I do not believe that a person who is driven by a compulsion they cannot control cannot be saved. I do believe that a person can be saved and resurrected with the rest of the saved even though they may die with a drink in their hand or a needle in their arm or during an immoral sexual act. Because sometimes people have compulsions that are beyond their ability to control. Christ knows your heart and does not judge as the world judges; His judgments are just.

The bigger stumbling block, in my experience, is belief. It is hard, after being brought up and living in a secular world to see with spiritual eyes (see 1 Corinthians 2:14; John 4:22–24). The worldly person just cannot see the things that are not visible to the eyes of flesh, and not being able to see, rejects them as foolishness (2 Corinthians 2:14–16). And the devil mocks those who do see. No one likes to be mocked and thought a fool. It is like the tale of the emperor's new clothes. I had to be *broken* to lose my barrier of pride, unbelief, and unspiritual worldly blindness. And yet, even now, Satan comes from all angles and tries in every way to cloud my vision. He is described as a serpent, but to me, he is a worm. He tries to come into my ear and mess with the machinery of my thoughts. For my heart is stronger; it is in the mind that he was lodged—by my father's and others' intellectualism and Marxist materialism. A worm, an evil parasite that looks to destroy the good by making it not.

Walking the Walk

As I told in *I, Witness*, these writings are not to tell you about me but rather to talk about Jesus Christ, to be a witness for Him. I am not an especially interesting person, nor necessarily a good person, but I am a *witness* to things that are of an extraordinary nature, of which some might benefit by reading. In law, a witness need not be special. I had a case once where the only eyewitness was a cognitively challenged individual. I argued that he should not be allowed to testify because he was so impaired that his testimony could be misleading and manipulated by the plaintiff's attorney and was of no value in understanding the facts. But the judge overruled me. Thus, I testify not that I am a great witness, but that because of these events I am a *witness*. I was in the place at the time when things transpired as they did for His glory who makes all things work according to His plan.

After my experience, I was in the office, and my doctor heard my tearful confession to her, and her words were these: "This is real salvation." She invited me to join with the believers in assembly and, with her husband, baptized me by immersion. And, God has been good because it was by His will that these things have been done. So, it was His plan for my life at this point that I volunteered at the shelter, and His plan that I joined the home church where I learned to study more deeply into the Bible.

I testified about my vision in our assembly, and the others told of visions they had had, and I realized that I was part of an assembly of people who had seen and who had heard things of God. Not that *anyone* is worthy in himself, but we are called by the will of God and the Holy

Spirit. He has taken those who were unworthy and has *made* us worthy by His power because we believe. And by the power in the blood, he has forgiven us. Amen (Let it be so).

Why was it so hard for me? I think there were three main reasons.

First, there were the arguments of my father, which were persuasive because he was a highly intelligent man. He convincingly spoke of the big bang theory and evolution and claimed religion was just stories made up to keep the "masses" in check. He thought most people unintelligent, ignorant, and in need of "smart" people to guide them and find solutions to social and economic problems.

Second was the weak version of Christianity taught in many mainstream churches, based on rules and conformity—which seems so incongruent with what I read in the Bible. For Christ died to free us from the law of sin and death and sent the Holy Spirit to be the guide and teacher of the saved. First-century Christians suffered a lot of persecution.

Third was the way "normal" people lived, accepting things like corruption, war, hate, and discrimination, which are obviously wrong. And the Church members were so obviously worldly and materialistic in their daily lives that it was hard to avoid the cognitive dissonance, constantly showing off in their nice clothes and fancy cars and big houses. Kids see that and compare what they see with what the Bible says. They see the way people treat the poor and other things that people do and say, "How can you claim that these people have been transformed?"

Modern people are afflicted with "existential neuroses," feeling at times elated by events in their lives like a new job or a new lover and at times depressed or suicidal because of the loss of them. They take the yin and yang events of life to heart ("Why am I a failure?" or "What is wrong with me that no one loves me?") They are suffering from shame, the fruit of the tree of the knowledge of good and evil because the phrasing of these questions goes to what one *is*, not to what one does.

A man at the shelter who is debating getting into treatment for alcoholism said, "I'm a drunk." But the truth is that he is *not* "a drunk." He is a *man* suffering from the compulsion to drink that he cannot control; it is the devil using his *shame* against him that stops him from coming to the one help that really exists. Why does this happen? How do people get into this trap, thinking "I am this" or "Why can't I?" or "What's wrong with me?" I was once there myself, and I think a huge part is focus and perspective. None of these things define what anyone is; they are the yin and yang, the ebb and flow of life. Some may relate to something a person does, but every single person is a *spirit*, created by God in His image (for He is spirit, John 4:24) and given a house of flesh.

Also, the point of view that puts oneself in the center and other people around him pulling this way and that *inevitably* causes imbalance. Because the spirit is weakened by the flesh and its wants, flawed, in all human beings, and other people are fickle, self-centered, and unbalanced in themselves. Thus, he who lives to himself alone, or if he lives to other people, is doomed at the outset to failure and confusion and more than that is subject to the manipulation of his inner being by falsehoods and lies, the fruit of the devil.

We all additionally develop 'personas' (the faces we show the world) to make others think we are doing better than we are, not being willing to just be seen as weak, fragile, naked, dying as we are living, impoverished even in wealth, lacking even though we have plenty, failing even in our success, fallible and frail and blind. Without the saving grace of Jesus Christ, that is the result of a secular life (see Revelation 3:17). And we are taught from birth to hide that fact and to pretend as everyone around us is pretending. The twelve-step programs are successful in part because they begin with accepting the reality and admitting it to oneself and to others.

So, what if Christ—the stone that is the foundation of everything—is the center, what, then, does the person's life look like? And if success is not measured with worldly eyes but in the sacrifice of ourselves to serve Him, how do we rate? And if we believe Romans 12:1—that life is *about* personal sacrifice and *not* achievement—and that He counts our worth by seeing into our depth, how then do we rate?

And if we believe the Beatitudes—that humility and peacefulness are the things for which we live—and money and possessions are *nothing*— what then is there to be depressed about? In the 1980s, I remember people saying, "Whoever dies with the most toys wins the game!" But he who dies with the most toys, still believing that they are something, is overcome with grief at losing everything.

Christ *is* the center. We exist only to serve. This is why we were put here and why our failures are less important than our hearts. For He is the judge not as the world judges, but He sees to the depths of our hearts and our minds and our souls. So, success, as measured by the world, is nothing. Genuine success is not measured by an external measure that asks, "How many?" or "How much?" but by a heart gauge that asks, "How sincerely?" or "How unselfishly?" or "How humbly?" And every worthwhile thing we do is done in His name, and with love, because love is the greatest virtue (1 Corinthians 13:13).

A life without a solid, immovable center is a life at risk, not just a risk in a spiritual future but a risk here and now. This is Because things happen, and they are sometimes not pleasant or nice or pretty. People's family members die suddenly, sometimes horrifically. I know people whose families have been murder victims. People get cancer, and sometimes it is brutal. People work a lifetime and build something and invest everything into it and then lose it all in one day, as we have seen during the economic shutdown. Evil people victimize good people. There is rape and child abuse. People lie, cheat, steal, and betray friends and family. These things are catastrophic. Victims without a strong center can fall apart, turn to drugs or alcohol, or kill themselves. I have known about a dozen over a lifetime who have killed themselves. I do not believe they are automatically condemned, but I can't help thinking we failed them.

Also, there is permanent psychological harm. Victimization over time—mental, physical, and sexual cruelty. And it leaves deep scars that can last a lifetime. There are orphans and children of broken or nonexistent homes. And often, they are broken and lost from the start. They wind up in the shelters, on the street, or in prison. Often, they are half-socialized, unable to cope. They turn to alcohol and drugs to kill the pain. And many mental illnesses also result from all this destructive behavior.

I do not know if there are people who are simply unable to come to believe because they are too broken. But I can say that it has been my experience that whatever problems a person has, faith in Christ makes the person stronger and better able to cope with it, but only if they are properly taught to expect trouble and loss and suffering. So, when troubles come, the Christian person should immediately look for God's hand and seek to understand how He might use this as an opportunity for spiritual growth (I know from experience that this is hard and that the devil really tries to knock us off that track). But he should think about how he should respond in accordance with Biblical teaching and struggle against becoming angry, bitter, vengeful, or depressed and anxious, knowing God is still with us and we are being tested and refined for the kingdom. He or she might rely on the full armor of God (Ephesians 6:10–18). Ruminating excessively about whatever happened in the past is pointless. Finding a way to serve God in new or adverse circumstances is much more fruitful. It still hurts, and it is still really hard, but it is not pointless, which is the key to understanding.

Three quarters of a century ago, there arose in Europe the philosophy of existentialism, positing that there is no God, that man defines himself by his deeds, and that life is "absurd" because of the "unexplained" suffering of human beings. We are therefore like Sisyphus, condemned to endless toil with no purpose, followed by a final death and nothing else (no God, meaningless existence, final death). Albert Camus suggested that in this situation, the only real question was whether to commit suicide.

But, given that there is a divine, intelligent Creator, there is meaning in suffering. There is an afterlife, there is an eternal essence, and those things we see as evil really are evil. It all changes, and if so, we live not for ourselves but for that which is greater than ourselves. Further, we must exist not merely for other people but for that which is greater than other people as well. Then, we will have a life that is stable, at least to the extent that, as long as we are faithful, it does not fall apart at every bump in the road because our center cannot hold, and it does not come undone because of the constant pushing and pulling by others. We love them, we help them, but we live for Him. Then and only then does life and death, suffering and toil, make sense. Then, even Sisyphus can find rest.

One beautiful thing about the mind is that we can truly focus on only one thing at a time. So, when we are focused on serving the Lord and on serving our fellow man, we necessarily focus less on ourselves, and our problems start to fade into the background. Now, if I am bleeding, it may be good to focus on that immediately. But if I have cancer, what good does it do me to focus on that all the time? If I am bankrupt, there may be some immediate tasks that need doing, but to ruminate 24/7 on my situation is a path to depression and suicide. If I am afraid of the future, I need something present to focus on. Otherwise, anxiety may overwhelm me. If I have guilt about my past deeds, I need a way to be relieved of that burden.

I have found that all these kinds of problems are possible to endure with faith.[67] I believe that twenty-first-century man's real problem is in part loss of conscious awareness of why we were planted here in the first place. We are God's field, and the good grain awaits the harvest. We are the fruit of His vineyard and are ready for plucking and making into new wine. And if we focus on him as saved people, we will bear fruit.

But even those who do not believe that, if you are being serious, you must see that there really is nothing else in this world solid enough and reliable enough to hold onto when the sifting and shaking comes in earnest. At that time, the saved person of faith has something solid and permanent to hold onto. One without it has nothing that cannot be just snatched away in an instant by the quake, the storm, the plague, or the flood. Or by evil men.

Family die, friends desert, homes and wealth are lost; nations and kingdoms fall. None of it that cannot be here today, gone tomorrow. Our bodies age, our looks desert us. All that is worldly dies. What good is any of it when faced with imminent death? Christ, only Christ, remains standing when all else fails.[68] The solid rock upon which to build a life worth living at any age, any time. I know in my case it was hard because I knew a light or easy Christianity, which did not require much and didn't prepare me adequately for the hard realities of life. Maybe that was my own fault; I do not know. I do know I was not unique.

---

[67] I have to admit that there are some challenges I have not faced. There is no way to know how faith will hold up until it is tested. I have not had to endure death of a child, torture or total debilitating illness. All we can do is pray that our faith will hold and ask God to stay with us. We prepare by giving up as much as we can of worldliness and becoming more spiritual people. We understand that death and loss and suffering are baked in.

[68] See Ecclesiastes 12:1–14.

Living in the Spirit

Now in our discussion about shame we showed that the result of eating the fruit of the tree of the knowledge of good and evil was shame. For before eating, Adam and Eve were naked and unashamed, just like every creature God had made. But as soon as they ate, their eyes were opened, and they saw that they were naked, and they were ashamed. Furthermore, the Bible does not say they felt guilty for their disobedience. Guilt is remorse for what we do, but shame is directed to what we are. Being ashamed of what one is can be very destructive. If you look at Genesis 2:25, 3:7, and 3:10 all these passages say they *were* naked. "Were" is a form of the verb "to be." It implies more than something transitory. The author could have said they didn't have any clothes or something like that, but he clearly thought that to *be* naked was significant—in this case, the difference between innocence and shame that follows the loss of innocence.

I looked in the mirror as a child and wished I looked different, saw myself as ugly and defective, inferior to other people and this is the effect of shame. Many people experience shame because of the cruelty of the world. When a child is a victim of cruelty, he or she internalizes this and believes there is something wrong with him. He may assume he is ugly, defective, inferior, unacceptable, or "bad." This may be one factor leading so many abused children into a life of addiction, homelessness, or other negative outcomes.

And what did the first people do? They made coverings for themselves out of leaves, and they hid themselves. People experiencing shame now still do the same thing. We cover ourselves with expensive clothes, with false smiles, with false laughter, with bravado, with false personas; all to hide our shame. Not only from others but even from ourselves. We call these things "defenses," and sometimes they break down, and we take anesthetic medicines to cope with the pain of shame.

Therefore, shame *is* poisonous to the spirit. Now, there are things in the world that are poisonous to the flesh so that if you eat them, you may die. But there are also things that are poisonous to the spirit so that they weaken the spirit and prevent a person from receiving God's greater gifts. If you read 1 Corinthians 2:10—16, you will see that Paul sets forth the result of an unspiritual life. This is also part of what the Lord referred to in John 9, when he said he had come into the world for judgment, to take sight from the seeing and give sight to the blind. But no one can have spiritual sight unless they are walking in the spirit with the one who made us. Who did Adam and Eve hide from in the garden? From God! We can't really hide from God, but we displease Him when we try, like Jonah. And this separates us from God.

This lack of spiritual sight is also part of the problem Nicodemus had with grasping the concept of being born again in John 3. Now, Nicodemus was a Pharisee, a man whose life was dedicated to studying the Scriptures of the "Old Testament." Jesus pointed out that all the Scriptures in the law and the writings of the Prophets spoke of Him, yet the priests and the Pharisees did not (for the most part) believe Him. If you reread the parable of the wedding feast in Matthew 22, you might consider these priests and teachers of the law were the invited guests who refused to attend. Sight requires obedience and humility, not pride and worldliness.

Because of their worldliness, the priests and Pharisees were spiritually blind. Paul says it plainly in Romans 8:5: "The mind governed by the flesh is death, the mind governed by the Spirit is life and peace" (see also Romans 8:13—14). "For those who are led by the Spirit of God are the children of God." Without the spiritual eyes being opened, what is left? The physical world, materialism, noise and distraction and every misfortune to which the flesh is subject. Without Spirit, this is all we can see. This then leads to greed, lust, and hate, based on the contest for stuff—all made of the mud of the earth as are the bodies of flesh. This is the way of despair and death.

In Jesus's time, accepting the coming of the Messiah would have meant that the priesthood would have had to give up their worldly positions. They would have had to surrender their power and wealth and honor here in the world and humble themselves before Him, a poor peasant from the despised Nazareth, a place of dishonor, the "wrong side of the tracks."

Probably not all the Pharisees were selfish or greedy. But the really dedicated ones, like Saul, who later became Paul, were immersed in their rules and traditions. Following rules blindly is another symptom of the lack of spiritual sight. Look at 2 Corinthians 3:4–18. The Pharisees studied the words chiseled in stone all day long. "For the letter kills but the spirit gives life" (2 Corinthians 3:6, in part). Recall how Jesus spoke to the Samaritan woman at Jacob's well, saying "The hour is coming and is now here when the true worshipers will worship the Father neither on this mountain nor in Jerusalem" (John 4:21).[69] Why is this important? Because the Torah is specific. The Hebrews of old had to travel to the place designated by God on festival days and to make the sacrifices commanded in Leviticus, and there was no other way to maintain the covenant they had made in Exodus 19. So now, Jesus said, "God is spirit, and his worshipers must worship in spirit and in truth" (John 4:24).

Paul says in Romans 7:6 "But now, by dying to what once bound us, we have been released from the law, so that we serve in the new way of the Spirit, and not in the old way of the written code." So, if we worship neither on the mountain nor in Jerusalem, where is the worship held? There are two answers based on these Scriptures. One says, "Anyplace, any time." Jesus can come to you in the prison cell, the dirty littered alleyway, the foxhole, especially. The other answer: "The human heart." Worship in spirit and in truth; Jesus dwells in the hearts of those who know Him. Amen.

I know our suffering is the crucible in which we are being refined for His kingdom. (I don't like pain and suffering any more than you do, which I was reminded of in my recent hospital visit with lots of both.) However, I know Christ is my only real hope. I pray to walk in His footsteps. I am neither strong nor brave, but by *His* grace, I pray the

---

[69] Jews were forbidden from associating with Samaritans.

Spirit lends me those qualities when needed. And I must be humble like Him and like Paul, a place where I most often fail and need His help.

So do not ask for miraculous cures for me. Pray to strengthen my faith, to fill me with grace. Pray to make me stand when I cannot stand so I finish my race strong. Pray that I use all this life until I use it up. Pray that I "leave it all on the field"; that I reach the goal with my last gasp. Pray, then, Jesus sees me like the widow who gave her last two copper coins, all she had (Luke 21:1–4). This is the way to the Kingdom. Not because of a command or out of duty but out of love. Amen.

All-In

If you ever played poker, you are familiar with that phrase. It is when a player pushes in his whole stack on a single bet. Jesus expects us to be all in for Him. He gave his all—flesh and blood—for us, suffering an agonizing death.

He says it clearly in Matthew 10: 37–38. If you love your family too much to be all in, you are out. When I first heard that, I thought it was terribly unfair. He says if you seek your life, you will lose it, but if you lose it for His sake, you will find it. Ouch.

I have found a certain liberation in having cancer. A freedom from many fears I used to have. In my foolish pride, I thought, "I'm not afraid of anything anymore!"

God heard that. Then my dearest love had a scare. Actually, she is not easily scared. I was scared. This morning, I had to come to terms with that. Begging, rationalizing, and finally, broken, taking the pain that I *could* lose her. My T-shirt was soaked with tears and snot dribbles, and my pride was put back in its box for now.

Everything goes at the foot of the cross! Our own lives, our possessions, easy, but also our relationships with our spouses and children and parents and whatever else we hold dear. We must take up our cross and follow! No matter how much it hurts!

So, in my mind I must consider laying my love at the foot of the cross, entrusting Jesus to take care of her, the brightest of jewels in my galaxy, bone of my bones and flesh of my flesh. It will hurt, gently, gently stroke her hair, wrap her feet, wash her face with my tears.

This may never come to happen, but if it does, a servant of Christ must accept it. And pride aside, it is what I fear most. I am laying bare my heart here.

Jesus, I pray whenever I am tested send the Holy Spirit to guide me. And when I am tempted send your angels to lead me away to a safe place. I am weak, but I would stand, for I know that you have power to make me stand. Amen.

So, Jesus does not accept halfhearted, lukewarm followers. As he said to the Laodicean church in Revelation, "Because you are lukewarm—neither hot nor cold—I am about to spit you out of my mouth" (Revelation 3:16).

How could it be clearer? As followers of Christ, we must pick up our crosses and follow him (Luke 14:27). When you are carrying your own cross to be crucified, there is no middle ground. You are either in or you are out. When we are tested, as many in this world are tested, with a gun to our temple, with evil men demanding that we renounce Jesus Christ, how will we respond? Because there are hundreds of people daily undergoing this exact test. In one recent year, it was estimated that over 100,000 people were martyred worldwide for Christ. These people, through faith, have found their peace with Him. Will we? Or are we so attached to the world, to the physical, to the things we see with the eye and feel with the skin that it is *impossible* for us to imagine giving up everything—our possessions, our money, our automobile, our house, and our very life? These are not merely theoretical. This is actually happening today, and Americans are not immune; it just feels that way because we are used to being safe. Ask a soldier, ask a first responder. This is a fact of life, and it is for a Christian also. You may never have a gun on you telling you to renounce your faith, but you might lose your job or other things you really care about for speaking up for what is right. Apparently, these days the worldly powers can persecute people even to the point of putting you in prison if they don't like you.

We live in America, probably the safest place on earth. This was a fortuitous fact for us. It has been the case because America was founded in faith. However, America, to quote President Obama, is no longer a Christian country. If America is no longer a Christian country, how do we have any right to expect that there is still a hedge of protection around it for our benefit? It is true that we have the strongest military in the world right now. So did Rome 2,000 years ago. So did Great Britain 300 years ago. In the interim, the world's most powerful military has been held by Spain, France, the Austro-Hungarian Empire, the Ottoman Empire, and many others. Where are they now? Empires of men are doomed from the start to fall. If God destroyed Israel because of transgressions 700 years before Christ, what makes us think we are exempt?

So, it is practically a foregone conclusion that our children or our children's children will also face trials like the trials faced by the citizens of failed empires. The *only* hope anyone has in this world is God, through Jesus Christ. And God has revealed Himself in the person of Jesus Christ to us with promises that are better and more perfect than the promises of worldly emperors or leaders or any other thing that might be in the world.

We can be saved from our mistakes and transgressions simply by believing in Jesus Christ and surrendering our lives to him. All he demands in return is *everything* we have in this world (see Luke 14:26–33). Before you start thinking that is unfair, remember that he gave everything he had in this world for us; and what he had in this world was everything there is. For the devil tempted him in this way by revealing that he could have *everything* in this world (Matthew 4:8–10). However, He resisted that temptation and suffered death on the cross instead out of obedience to the one and only God. So, he asks nothing of us that He would not suffer and give of Himself.

Taking the Challenge

Even after all this, in some ways I was still blind. I did not realize until recently the breadth and depth of the spiritual starvation in our Christian land. But, being first preoccupied with my own salvation experience, with relearning God's word, and with serving the poor to whom I was called by the Holy Spirit; and then the enormous task of writing and publishing my story, I had not been paying attention to the events going on in the world. Oh, I had expected the homeless to be needy, spiritually as well as in every other way, but as I push out the Gospel message that the Spirit gives me, using the reach of social media, I have gotten tearful messages and salvation stories and people hurting needing a place to turn. I know I must try to do something for them. I pray God keeps me here long enough to do my bit of it. No one mortal can do it all, only Jesus.

I have accepted that I have to face my own death, and ask the Holy Spirit for grace when the time comes. I do not want to leave undone that which God has given me to do. I pray that I don't spare myself anything to avoid all God has prepared for me. I expect that at some point, there will be more physical suffering, and that I will be tempted by it. But I am here for a purpose, and if you are reading this, so are you.

There are lots of people talking about God, about church, about the Bible. Some of them are truly called and sent out with power of the Holy Spirit, like the man born blind. Some are not. But there are nowhere near enough for all the starving spirits out here. I have spoken to people at all strata of our multilayered society, from the homeless to the lawyers and doctors, the winners, and the losers. And they, often, have either rejected what they call "religion " or have accepted the weak tea they serve at (some? most?) mainstream churches and think that's all there is. But the answers are in the Bible. "Unless your righteousness exceeds that of the Pharisees and the priests, you will not enter the kingdom of heaven" (Matthew 5:20). Read closely Matthew chapters 5 and 6. Set aside the arguments about following the law of Moses and *think* about how Jesus says we should live. Jesus fulfilled the law for us if we have the Holy Spirit.

Consider the Beatitudes as if they were commandments of God (they are!).[70]

Consider conquering the desires of your flesh (lust, etc.) to be mandatory. Because these powerful fleshly desires pull people away from the Spirit. At a minimum, they are to be fully exhausted in a Godly way with the partners God gave us. (In my past life, I failed here.) Desire is of the flesh, and it would be your master, but we are called to master desire so that our only master will be Christ (see Genesis 4:6–7). Consider turning the other cheek to be both a duty and a privilege (it is). Consider it essential to be *ready* to let go of your parents, spouses, siblings, even children, at any time, to lay them at the foot of the cross, amid tears of parting and farewells. Consider anger, revenge, and hate to be strictly forbidden, even to those who harm you, and forgiveness and loving your enemies to be required (they are). Consider pride to be poison, whether pride in your body, or your possessions, which is idolatry—or in your accomplishments or in your piety (a failing of mine, at times).

And, at this point, you should be on your knees before the Lord either physically or in spirit. I am—for I know I cannot do all this—yet I must. What I am saying is the weak teaching says that these are "merely aspirational," but I am saying Christ meant every word as *imperative*. Not merely that, but that these are the *minimum* standard, and that through living this way and persistent prayer, we reach an even *higher*

---

[70] Not to create more guilt. Christ *died* to take away guilt. But that does not mean He didn't intend for us to try. And no, it's not "salvation by works." But that doesn't mean faith does not require action. We listen to the Holy Spirit; we live as children of light; we love one another, love other people and even love our "enemies." Works flow naturally from these things.

standard of a spiritual life, led by the spirit and by faith in Yeshua in *everything* we do and say. Not that any of us complete the journey in life, but we keep fighting. And, of course, we have the limitations of the flesh. So, therefore, we fail, and the devil tries to convince us that we can't do it—it's a fool's errand—and to give up.

"But God chose the foolish things of the world to shame the wise" (1 Corinthians 1:27). So, okay, you failed. God says, "Get up! Now go fail again. Fail over and over. In failing you will succeed."

Paul traveled around the Middle East and Asia Minor and what is now Turkey with nothing but what he could carry. He came to town and went immediately to the synagogue and began to preach Jesus Christ (see Acts 13, 19). Often, he was rejected. He suffered beatings and floggings and once was stoned and left for dead. He was shipwrecked. He would go "first to the Jew and then to the gentile" (for example, Acts 19: 8–10). If he failed with the Jews, sometimes the Gentiles accepted him. Sometimes he was chased out of town by an angry mob. He was arrested in Jerusalem. Often, he failed to convert people with his Gospel. Ultimately, he was beheaded. The Apostles were willing to fail and fail again and again. And billions of people follow their example. Now go start failing! The reward is for those who persevere (Romans 8:5:3–5, Revelation 2:26–28). Paul speaks of his struggles with sin in Romans 7, Peter's sins included denying Christ out of fear. We bless those who try and fail as much as those who succeed because God does not judge as the world judges.

For he who never lost never really took on anything too difficult (i.e., he played it safe), and he who never failed never really succeeded. Failing is how our eyes are opened; it is how our spirits grow. Fail enough and you will win.

This is the place the Holy Spirit enters and carries us to the goal. We have to pray for the Holy Spirit to be in us, to fill us, to give us its "superpowers," to enable us to continue to try even when we fail. Superpowers like the will to be bold as never before, letting go of the safe place and challenging every obstacle, praying constantly to the Holy Spirit that He will sustain us in every effort, giving us courage and strength even as our own are failing us.

In fact, without the Holy Spirit we are powerless. The power comes from God not from us (Ephesians 6:10–20). We must be willing to try to do the things we are afraid of. We have to be willing to fail. We must be humble to accept our failure and try again. This is the life to which Christ calls us. It is both exhilarating and terrifying at the same time! Do we accept the challenge? That is the calling of Christ.

What Is It That Christ
Is Demanding of Us?

He wants us to be worthy. He knows that we cannot completely succeed in this. He knows our weaknesses, our failures, our sins, our transgressions, our mistakes. There is no fooling him. He sees our hearts. He sees right through us. Confession is more admitting our failure to ourselves and others because Christ already knows, and He accepted us by dying for us on the cross. What greater sign of acceptance could there ever be? So even if you have not yet been saved, if you are reading this, you are not beyond hope! "No one can come to me unless the Father who sent me draws them, and I will raise them up at the last day" (John 6:44). So, if you are a seeker, the fact you are still reading this means you are coming to Him; the Father who sent Him is calling you, and if you surrender to Him right now, you will be raised! Alleluia!

What are we to do? Look at the opening verses of Romans 6. In Baptism, the believer dies and is buried with Christ. He arises a new creation in Christ, animated by the Holy Spirit. Does that mean he doesn't ever sin? No, it means that he does not *intentionally* sin. He doesn't *set out* to do things that he knows are wrong. In Romans 7, Paul describes his own struggle with sin. It is a blessing that this chapter is included in our Bible today. Because we have a similar struggle with sin, each of us in our own life. Sin is still with us because we are living in a body of flesh in a sinful world. Sometimes we cannot resist temptation, sometimes we are under compulsions that we cannot control, and sometimes we do not realize that something we say or do is prideful until after we've done it.[71] Sometimes we respond in anger without thinking. Sometimes we hurt other people without meaning to. Sometimes our vision of ourselves or of our own behavior is clouded by a lifetime of deception created by the devil. No man, while living, can completely overcome all these evils.

But what Jesus does expect, is that if you realize something would be dishonest or wrong before you do it, you are strictly forbidden to do it. I was recently tempted in this way, but alarm bells went off in my head and I was able to stop myself before I went through with it. And although my motives were the best, my action would have been evil. This is where the "little white lie" is so deadly. For we know that the devil is the author of lies and the father of lies and that when he lies, he speaks his native language (see John 8:44). Therefore, we who belong to Him must not lie, even "little white lies" with pure motives. We must not take what is not ours regardless of why we want it or how trivial it is. When we say to ourselves, "I'm going to go over there and give those people a piece of my mind," it is well to take a moment and reflect whether Christ would approve. It is good if we think ahead of time and stop ourselves before we carry through this action so we do not harm anyone and we do not respond in anger. When we think, *Aha! I have done well!* it would be well for us to think, *I am a sinner; this was the work of the Holy Spirit, acting through me, and not me myself.*

All these things are incidents of *temptation to sin* that we have the ability to stop before they occur. *When we resist, we recapitulate the temptation of Christ in Matthew 4.* This is part of walking in His footsteps! It is another proof one is on the right track. If we fail, we recall the times Peter failed. And then, we can pray for God's help through the Holy Spirit to avoid such failures in the future. Thus, while we are all sinners and no one can be perfect, we can, day by day, put forth our greatest effort to be the person Christ would have us to be. We do this in all humility, *knowing* that we will fail before we begin. Even in writing these books, there are *moments* of failure. By this, I mean there are moments of pride and self-glorification that I must go back and reflect and pray about. There are also moments

---

[71] Some words have left my mouth that I wish I could take back. It is painful.

of bitterness. Thanks be to God our Father, who has sent us His Holy Spirit to guide us and empower us and to teach us all things. And he has given us the written record, not as the old covenant on tablets of stone but as a better covenant written on the human heart (2 Corinthians 3:4–11). Therefore, we are empowered to go to the places where we can shine the light of Christ and become a beacon to people who are lost. And we can be fountains of salvation, for as Christ Jesus spoke, "He who believes in me as the Scripture said, rivers of living water will flow from within them. By this he meant the spirit, whom those who believed in him were later to receive" (John 7:38–39). "But their minds were made dull, for to this day the same veil remains when the old covenant is read. … But whenever anyone turns to Christ the veil is taken away" (2 Corinthians 3:14–16).

When we accept Christ Jesus as our Lord and Savior, the veil is lifted and we who were blind see (2 Corinthians 3:16, John 9:39–40). The Gospel is still veiled to those who are perishing because the devil has blinded them (2 Corinthians 4:3). This is also because people who are unspiritual cannot understand what must be spiritually discerned (1 Corinthians 2:10–15). "Okay, Joe, that's a nice Bible lesson, but how does this play out in our real lives, and why is it important?"

Here is why it's important. All the temptations of the devil are designed to distract our attention. I discovered this when I started spending more time alone with God. And many people have a hard time seeing and understanding the spiritual because of this. Does the Bible seem opaque at times? Are there aspects of faith that are hard to understand? This is true for everyone to greater or lesser degrees. This is in part because of distractions and lack of focus.

There are the temptations of the flesh, not only sex but food, nice things, pleasing things, anything that one may focus on. Why? And advertising, seemingly endless streams of unwanted information. Why is it a problem?

Because our little 3-pound brain can only focus on one thing at a time. And it takes one's whole brain to focus on the spiritual reality to understand it. You can't do it in little snippets or even in a thirty -minute church sermon. That is why the Israelites were given a Sabbath day. They were farmers and worked long hard days. Toil was their lifestyle. We live in a different world. But you need at least a couple of hours undistracted several times a week to enter God's rest. See Hebrews chapters 3 and 4. I'm not saying you shouldn't keep the Hebrew Sabbath if you can, if you are convinced that is right. But what I am saying is that it is not a "rule" to create guilt; it is a *practice* to create a spiritual state of mind so that you can get away from worldly distractions.

The devil puts so many of these in our paths to keep us blind. Internet pornography is one, as it is highly addictive. Facebook is another if it is used incessantly to post inane and ridiculous trivia all day. I never turn it on until after my "God time." Tasks, our jobs, homes, and kids take us away from the special time we require to find God, as well as anger and irritation, vexatious calls, traffic, nasty comments on Twitter, the frustrations of the world, and 99 percent of the stuff on TV. The point is, it doesn't matter what is keeping us away from God. It only matters that we spend *enough* time with Him to see in the spirit. When we keep the channel open, he will teach us all things and empower us, and through us, others. We each become reflectors of His light to the world, even in our imperfection, because His light is perfect, and we are just a reflector for Him. It is the Holy Spirit shining *through* us that is the light if we are obedient to it. I have to admit I am not always able to do this myself, but as broken as I am, I am trying.

I can testify that spending time with God and trying to follow Jesus's example is how I manage to live as I do, despite advanced cancer, despite age, despite treatments, despite distractions, obstacles, fears (I'm human) and all the other things that would stop me. And I spread the Gospel in the homeless shelter, on the Internet, and in the book I wrote; or rather, the Holy Spirit works through me to show the glory of Jesus Christ to the world, at least some of it, as well as possible for I am a leaky vessel at best. But through Him, all things are possible. And He has used me as a carpenter uses a hammer and saw to do His will.

In practical terms, I, Joe, advise anyone to find yourself a time. Spend that time alone with the Bible, a pen, and some paper. Read, pray, and keep a journal. Require everyone to let you alone during this time. Shut out noise and distraction as much as possible. Early morning or late at night works best, but whatever works for you. If done with patience and perseverance, eventually, you will open your God channel, your spiritual eyes, and things *will* become clear for you in time. What is hidden will be revealed, and what is invisible will become visible. You will receive messages and callings and comforts in the spirit. Fears, anxiety, and worries will diminish, and your power to act in His name will gradually grow.

We Are Blessed—Be Happy!

Okay, I understand the country, and God's people, and the rest are going through a crisis in 2021. Evil seems to be ahead on points right now. We have to be serious about that. And it is not wrong to be patriotic. It is hard because so many fine people have given so much, including some of my best friends. But we can't turn our backs on who we are. Let me say it again. We can't turn our backs on who we are. We are the body of Jesus Christ on earth.

Read, or reread Romans 12–15. These chapters were included to explain Christian life to new Christians, but they are the fundamentals of how we are to *be*. Do we react constantly to worldly events and politics and news? Is that biblical? (I ask these questions rhetorically because some of my friends are so wound up in this.) Are we angry? Are we terrified? We are to be peaceful, humble, kind, prayerful. If we oppose something and believe it is from the devil, we pray about it. If someone offends us, we forgive them. If a brother or sister sins, we exhort them to see their error and pray for them.

We owe no one anything but the duty of love (Romans 13:8–10). Does Christian love harm anybody? No. We don't need rules to tell us not to hurt our loved ones. We have to be aware, Christian love is not "romantic" love, and sexual immorality is forbidden! But always remember the gifts we've been given and that we are commanded to love one another as brothers and sisters in Christ.

Jesus Christ gave His precious blood for us to free us from sin, guilt, punishment, and the awful burdens of shame and all the other things we carry on our hearts. He carried them on His cross so that our hearts would be free. He showed this to me in a vision, but it is also for you! He took the "weight of the world" on His cross because He could! It's what He died to do!

Therefore, the kingdom of God is not about [worldly matters]; it is about a righteousness that is a free gift (see Romans 3–4). It is also about joy! And peace in the Holy Spirit (Romans 14:17). Therefore, be filled with peace; show peace to all people with whom you have contact in your daily life (see John 14:27, Romans 5:1). And so, rejoice, for the kingdom of heaven is at hand (see 2 Corinthians 6:2–10).

Look at Revelation 7:9–17. I do not deny that the tribulation in Revelation is a real event but let me posit that the "great ordeal" has another meaning, and that is *life* and the suffering that goes with that. Hard times, hard knocks, times of poverty, times of plenty, new loves and bitter breakups, friends that desert and betray—all the stinging arrows of Satan we take in a lifetime. So many, so painful: war, flood, insults, defeats, suicides, and cancer. And our mistakes and transgressions and times when we are just too weak to do what He asks. But in our pain, if we turn to Christ, He cleans us from our mistakes, our shame, our guilt, the hurts we inflict upon one another, our habits that we cannot control, our drunken, lewd and obnoxious youth, our cowering self-preserving acts of dishonesty (think Peter's triple denial of Christ). All, every bit wiped clean so that we can stand in robes of white, joined as brothers and sisters with the Messiah, and we will not hunger or thirst, for the Shepherd will be in our midst always, and God Himself will wipe every tear from our eye. For Jesus told me in a vision that this is what He died to do, and if He did for me, an ordinary sinner, weak and worldly, then He also did for you. We can all drink from the fountain. *This is the good news and message of the entire Bible, the reason for all that happened, and it is good news for us all, all who just choose Him, believing, and grow their faith through work and suffering; through denying ourselves and putting others first in in His name and for His glory. Amen!*

So, I write these things boldly, but I want to focus attention on the glory we have today, in the Lord Jesus Christ. We have life eternal now (John 5:24). We are blessed above all people ever, and we should be happy in the knowledge we did nothing to be given a life in this world. It was a free gift. We did not nothing to deserve the gift of Christ's blood to save us from the consequences of our own mistakes. It was a free gift. We didn't earn it; we didn't deserve it. We just received it. What's not to be happy about?

Postscript

When I wrote *I, Witness*, I added a postscript. It was what was in my heart during one of our morning walks. Life was so beautiful, salvation so sweet. There was no COVID-19. The country prospered. We prospered. It was spring.

A lot has happened since that time. First the pandemic, then riots and the unbelievable destruction in several cities. Racial divisions I thought dead have been once again stirred up by the devil. We have seen on video people beaten to death, police cars burning, cities on fire.

And politics constantly barraging us with lies and propaganda, not just two sides but betrayals, corruption, and evil on both sides. And division and hate stirred up in our discourse. It is sickening. Sinful.

In my own life, as I mentioned, another cancer. I had been walking on air for almost three years. I dared to make plans, hope for the future, take for granted that God had given me time. Of course, all those plans and mental constructs have to go on the altar. My time here grows shorter.

I still serve those who are in need. The other night, I met one who is frightened with cancer or probable cancer. I have resolved to help her if I can. I have resolved to help as many as possible with all I have as well as I can, to give myself fully to Jesus Christ and the service of humanity and to hold back nothing. And to be humble, knowing I will soon face Him and praying He recognizes me and welcomes me. For I was a sinner.

But my hope is in Jesus, and it is a hope that does not disappoint, as Paul says. And therefore, I put all my hope in Him, and none in the world. Because to set my mind on the world is death; spirit and life are in Him alone.

So, the new wine of salvation has sobered up to the mature vintage of enlightenment. It's not all roses and unicorns. There is the cross. No way around. No way back. The only way is through. As I was waiting for a shot in the chemo room, one of the others said to me, "I guess we just have to walk it out."

But here is my prayer: "Jesus, I do not have the courage and strength to do this on my own. Please give me the grace to walk my walk as a servant. Lend me strength when I need strength. Lend me courage when I need courage. Give me grace when others need help, to serve them and ignore myself as You saved the thief, though Your hands and feet were spiked to the wood. I give everything into your safekeeping. That which is good, retain, that which is chaff throw out. You who suffered and died for me accept my suffering and death as if a sacrifice to your glory." Amen.

One more bit and a caution. I don't give a hoot how old the world is. And you can see I speak plainly because I am not trying to win anything or to deceive anyone with fancy talk. In the beginning, God created the heavens and the earth, that I believe. I don't worry much about predestination or other age-old controversies. I just don't have time. There is much to do, and I have two cancers—*Twice Blessed*. People want to argue about things on Facebook; I think it's fine if they are civil. I have been up in an airplane over the ocean and seen the curvature of the earth, so I can testify it is round, not flat. If anyone doesn't believe me, I can't help them.

I saw Jesus Christ in a vision. He is alive and well. And for the sinner in trouble, He will save *you* from the mess you probably have made of your life (or will eventually); if you have not met Him, you really should. He is the rock.

God still sends visions and dreams and revelations to people. He never stopped. People stopped listening and believing because of all the distractions of modern life and brainwashing in government schools. Few people can come to Him without first having the juice of pride crushed out of them in His winepress—our earthly suffering. But when they do, they will come to him on their knees because they will be facing something they don't know how to face (in my case, cancer) and have nowhere else to go. For this, we suffer and die. But it is a blessing. Just as a woman's birth pain, it is awful to go through but has a greater reward at the end than money, fame, or whatever else anyone might want in this temporary shell of flesh.

You and every single person you ever met, all your family, friends, children, everyone—are all doomed to die in the flesh, as am I, and I testify that for most, it will come too soon. Few are ready when it happens. But there is one hope in Christ Jesus. He is the Great High Priest of God Most High, Creator of Heaven and earth. If you come to Him in full surrender, you will live on and be raised at the last day, perfected and whole.

So, give me a grade.

I said there were four things I meant to do with this book:

- To explain in Biblical terms why people are "stuck" and how to be unstuck by making Christ the center of one's life;
- To explain God's one plan and to make the whole Bible easier to understand;
- To provide some ideas for really living the Gospel; and
- To explain why we have to suffer and die in the flesh.

Did I succeed for you? You are the judge.

Joe

Appendix I—God's Plan in a Nutshell

God is what we call the ultimate power that created the universe as we know it, that we see as intelligent and purposeful and has revealed Himself to us in many ways. He is known (in English) by other names such as Jehovah, Yahweh, YHWH, and just "I Am." And of course, He has names in other languages as well.

God's plans are perfect. He never makes mistakes. He is sovereign over all things.

God created man out of the stuff of the earth to be intelligent and gave him free will so that he could choose to worship and obey God voluntarily. Sometimes Man did not do as God desired because God allowed him to have free will. It was God's sovereign choice to give us free will and intellect, knowing full well that the devil will deceive some. And as Paul says, since man did not acknowledge God or worship Him, God, therefore, gave him over to "shameful lusts" and other evil, and death—both physical and spiritual—are the result. God knew from the beginning that some would not accept the call, but if you are reading this and *want* to come to Him, you *are* being called.

God's plan, knowing this, is Jesus Christ, His Son. That this was always planned is illustrated throughout the "Old Testament" and the whole Bible. See Ephesians 1:3–14. This is just one example that clearly sets forth God's *one* plan "from the foundations of the earth."

But first God created a place and a people to which he would send His Son. This was ancient Israel. It was for this that He called Abraham out of the desert; for this that He tested Abraham to see if he would sacrifice Isaac; for this that Joseph was sold to Egypt and then the whole family went to Egypt. It was for this that He brought the people out of Egypt after 430 years, and from there to Mount Sinai, where He gave them the law with fire and thunder. It was part of the plan that Israel and the temple of Solomon fell to Nebuchadnezzar and that the Second Temple was raised. And it was for this that the Priests' and Pharisees' hearts were hardened, and whose eyes were covered by a veil, so that they sacrificed Christ on the cross.

And the devil was tricked because God raised Christ from death, and He lives, and He saves those whom God calls. *All* who look to Him and believe in Him will be saved. He is the High Priest Forever who intercedes for all of humanity with God. Those who trust in Him will never be put to shame, and He will return in glory and raise up those who believe at the last day.

We who know Him are expected to live according to the teachings of Christ as fully as possible. We are to live the life of the Sermon on the Mount and to give all we have. Tokens are insufficient. And we are *guaranteed* suffering along the way. Our reward is eternal life. This is not "salvation by works"; true works of God flow *from* salvation naturally. If one is saved, the good works will follow naturally. And it is a sign of our salvation that we have a *genuine* love for one another and for other people. Even if you sell everything you have and give it all to the poor, it is meaningless if you do not have love (1 Corinthians 13:2). Christ commands us to love God and one another and all people. This is the sign of the Christian.

The things of the world are dross, rags, chaff. We must be purified by fire, which is the reason we suffer, and even if the devil is the author of our affliction, God will use it for our good if we are faithful like Job. Nothing is ever about what happens here; it is always about our response. We must be purged of worldliness and pride.

It is impossible to do all He demands on one's own, but He sent the Holy Spirit to help us and teach us and give us power. We have to spend daily time listening for God and preparing ourselves to meet life's challenges in a Spirit-directed way. It won't be perfect, but we can't give up. We try and fail and try again. This does not negate our salvation;

it *confirms* it. And we are to remain positive and joyful that He has arranged it so that all is for our good and our ultimate victory. He will return in glory to claim His own. Amen.

Everything in the Bible is intended to help us see and fully understand this, His plan, and to more fully know the mind of God. *It is all good news!*

Appendix II—Excerpt
from I, *Witness*

This is the vision I had and the reason I wrote I, Witness.

It was a regular day, although the cancer was always in the back of my mind. I was in my house and had just gotten dressed as I was leaving from the back bedroom and headed down the hall. I had been thinking and praying and my thoughts were that I was trying to love others, but it was hard to love Jesus, as I didn't really know Him. I also felt that certain sins from my past were weighing me down, and it was my feeling I would have to carry them for the rest of this life, and hope I was forgiven in the end. I know these are mixed up thoughts. Suddenly, I was seeing one of my past sins in high definition, as clearly as being there in the flesh. It was every gory detail. Exactly as it had really happened.

I was still aware that I was walking to the kitchen. Then another vision of a past event. It was very real. I was holding the kitchen counter, as I saw a third vision of another past event. I was re-living all my past sins, and the thoughts and feelings that went with them. The things I had used as defenses were stripped away. Justifications, excuses, and rationalizations no longer protected me from the pain. *I was being forced to face the evil;* to face the full weight of the harm to other people. Some were from childhood, some from adulthood. I saw them one after another.

Lies I had told, infidelities, sexual sin, mistakes covered up, cruelties, drunken, profane behavior. Things I said that I regretted. *I was seeing every ugly thing I had ever done in my past.* With each one a weight was added to my shoulders and my heart. It was very much like those lead vests they have in the x-ray room at the hospital. Weight kept piling on me. I had to sit down. I got over to my chair by the picture window in the living room, just a few steps from the kitchen, and sat down. The visions didn't stop. The weight didn't stop getting heavier. It felt like I was being crushed. It was hard to breathe. I squeaked out "Jesus, help me."

That is when I saw His Face, slightly above and to the left of me, as I was sitting there. The voice said either "I thought you were never going to ask" or "I thought you'd never ask." I am not certain which, they mean the same to me. The face appeared at first with emanations of red and yellow around it, as well as I can recall, just at the first. It was coming toward me.

I have the belief that the appearance of the face I saw could be what I needed it to be. I do not know. However, so that you may believe I am telling the truth, and hiding nothing, it was a handsome face with a square jaw, and black beard and hair, dark eyes, big square teeth. It was a handsome, tan face.

Then I saw Him directly in front of me and slightly above me. He said, in a normal voice, "Do me a favor and toss that up here on this cross I'm carrying." I looked down and my sins were in a brown cloth bag, or burlap. I now easily lifted them onto the cross. It was a large oversize wooden cross. He said "I'll carry them with me up to Calvary." I saw other things up there also, like the weight of the world. I thought it must be terribly heavy. I think He knew my thoughts. He turned to me and grinned, a regular full grin. Like "Yeah, I got this." And he was gone.

But he came back one last time in front of my face, and said "after all, it's what I died to do." And, once more, He was gone, taking my great weight with him.

The first thing I noticed was that the weight of sin I had carried, some of it 40, 50 and 60 years was gone. And it has never come back in the 20 months or so since, as of this writing. I can breathe. I am not weighed down by the past, by my baggage, by sin, none of it. It was taken and put to death on the cross, washed clean by the blood of Christ.

I do not worry about the cancer, about death, about suffering. In a way, I feel it is a privilege to suffer and die for the One who suffered and died for me. As I said, I am neither brave nor strong. But I have a real faith. A certainty of salvation and the world to come. *Christ Jesus lives. Alleluia.*

Then one more thing happened.

The Spirit led me to pick up my Bible and took me to a verse I had read many times, but like a man with a veil over his eyes, I had read it without comprehension. It is sandwiched in between miracles like walking on water and feeding 5,000 people with three loaves and two small fishes.

"I will tell you the truth, whoever hears my words and believes the one who sent me has eternal life and will not be condemned; he has crossed over from death to life." John 5:24 (NIV).

Here is how the Spirit showed me to read:

WHOEVER! (including me!)

"...hears my words ..."

"...and believes the one who sent me ..." (yes, I believe because of what I saw)

"...HAS eternal life ..." (i.e., RIGHT NOW, present tense)

"...and will NOT be condemned ..." (future tense, do not be afraid, you are ok)

; (semicolon) (next part)

He HAS crossed over from death to life! (past tense, it is done).

Past, present, future ... the trinity of time!

Here is part of why this is so important: first, it does not matter WHY I believed. The fact is THAT I believed in Him. And because I believed, I have eternal life. The Greek word used, I looked this up, also means spirit life, as well as eternal life. I was dead, and like the Prodigal Son; now I am alive! It was done by the power of Jesus Christ, because I was truly *repentant*, sorry for the past, and honestly intending never to do *any* of those things again; because I *asked;* and because I *believe* in Him, who I saw in the vision.

I know that what I saw was truth, because when I saw those sins, every one of them was true, *exactly* as it happened. They were far more realistic and awful than ordinary memories. I know everything I saw of Christ was right, *because the admission of guilt and conviction of sin preceded it*, and because everything is consistent with the Bible. I was fully awake and aware of my surroundings, so I know it was a vision, not a trance or stupor. I was wide awake, so I know it was not a dream. And it was *effective*, because the weight has not returned, though writing parts of this story have revived some unpleasant memories.

"*For I will forgive their wickedness and I will remember their sins no more.*" Jeremiah 31: 34 (NIV).

"*Then they cried out to the Lord in their trouble, and he saved them from their distress.*" Psalm 107:19 (NIV)

Kim Webb, Executive Director of the Emergency Shelter of Northern Kentucky, swings sledgehammer to start construction of a permanent low barrier shelter for our area. Donate at EmergencyShelterNKY.org

Author going to the river camps with supplies for the homeless

About the Author

Have you ever wondered why we have to suffer? Have you ever felt like you were "stuck" or never seem to be able to "get anywhere"? Or thought "life stinks"? Or maybe thought it was unfair that other people seem to be doing so well, and you have these problems?

Joseph was diagnosed with stage four cancer in 2016, and felt many of these same things. Then, by the grace of God and the Holy Spirit, he received a powerful vision of Jesus Christ that changed his life. Forgiven for all his sins and unchained from the past and the future, he has devoted his life to serving God and working with the homeless even through the pandemic, and written two books. The spirit also gave him additional insights into life and into scripture which are set out in language anyone can understand, as well as a simple explanation of the Bible that will help anyone seeking to uncover its greater gifts with prayer and study.

Printed in the United States
by Baker & Taylor Publisher Services